PRIVATE CONFESSIONS

INGMAR BERGMAN was born in Upsala, Sweden, in 1918. He started his career in motion pictures in 1944, and made his début as a director with *Crisis* (1945). He achieved international recognition with such films as *Summer with Monika*, *Smiles of a Summer Night*, *The Seventh Seal*, *Wild Strawberries*, *The Virgin Spring*, *Fanny and Alexander* and many others. While he himself has won several major film awards, his novel *The Best Intentions* won the Palme d'Or at the Cannes Film Festival in its screen version directed by Bille August. *Sunday's Child* was made into a film by the author's son Daniel Bergman. He has written and produced plays as well, and is author of an autobiography, *The Magic Lantern*.

JOAN TATE is the translator of Bergman's *The Best Intentions* and *Sunday's Child*, and *The Magic Lantern*, as also of a great number of Sweden's leading writers. Her work has been recognised with an award from the Swedish Academy.

Ingmar Bergman

PRIVATE
CONFESSIONS

*Translated from the Swedish
by Joan Tate*

THE HARVILL PRESS
LONDON

First published in Sweden with the title *Enskilda Samtal*
by Norstedts Förlag, Stockholm, 1996

First published in Great Britain in 1996
by The Harvill Press,
84 Thornhill Road,
London N1 1RD

First impression

A CIP catalogue record for this book is available
from the British Library.

The publishers gratefully acknowledge the financial support of the
Swedish Institute towards the publication of this book in English.

ISBN 1 86046 211 1

Designed and typeset in Janson at
Libanus Press, Marlborough, Wiltshire

Printed and bound in Great Britain by Butler & Tanner
at Selwood Printing, Burgess Hill

Contents

First Conversation (July 1925)   3

Second Conversation (August 1925)   27

Third Conversation (March 1927)   54

Fourth Conversation (May 1925)   70

Fifth Conversation (October 1934)   96

Epilogue-Prologue (May 1907)   110

PRIVATE CONFESSIONS

First Conversation
July 1925

It is the last Sunday in July, 1925, a hot sunny afternoon in Stockholm. The church clock in the tower above the cupola strikes half past three. The streets are deserted. A tram is making its way laboriously up the hill along the west side of the churchyard bordering on the spacious square with its indoor market and theatre. At the stop, a woman gets off and stands there.

Anna.

She is wearing a beige suit, the ankle-length skirt a slightly darker colour, high-heeled boots and a simple shady hat. Her jacket is open over a white high-necked lace blouse. She is wearing no jewellery, except her wedding rings and small diamond ear-rings. She is clutching her pale leather handbag to her, her thin gloves carelessly thrust into the jacket pockets.

She takes off her hat and holds it in her left hand. Her thick dark hair is parted in the middle and gathered into a low knot that has begun to loosen. Her eyes are dark brown below the strongly drawn eyebrows and low broad forehead. Her mouth is large, the lips friendly and generous.

Anna.

For twelve years she has been married to Henrik, curate at the church with its majestic cupola and the clock that has just struck half past three. She is thirty-six and has three children, two boys and a girl.

She looks around and decides to take the route across the churchyard, perhaps sit on one of the green benches inside for a while in the fragrance of the linden trees, a little cool, to breathe.

As always, she moves quickly and purposefully, her head slightly bowed, glancing swiftly to the side. Deserted and silent, not a soul.

So she is frightened when someone calls out her name. She flushes violently and looks round.

Uncle Jacob.

He is sitting on a bench by the church wall, deep in the shade of the trees. He waves invitingly with his big hand. "Hullo, hullo, Anna dear. Come on over and sit down for a moment. You can't be in all that much of a hurry. Come on, then."

Uncle Jacob is a tall man with iron-grey, slightly unruly hair, a trim grey beard and moustache. High forehead, heavy large face, grey eyes, a largish nose and broad mouth with soft corners. His hands are large and shapely, with swollen veins and some irregular liver spots on them. His voice is deep, with a trace of an accent, Småland, I seem to remember. He is wearing his clerical garb, the thin grey summer coat and wide-brimmed hat lying on the bench. Jacob is sixty-four and has been the parish priest for twenty years. So he is Henrik's superior. Anna is given a pat on the cheek by that large hand. She makes a little bob and smiles uncertainly, trying to control her ungovernable feeling of being caught out.

But she has been caught out.

Jacob invites her to sit down beside him. They exchange rapid snippets of information, asking after the general state of health of their respective families. Jacob has come in from the country for a funeral. He also has evensong at six o'clock and has promised to assist at communion. On Monday he will be going out to Maria, who is quite well now after recovering from a lengthy chill. He is going out to the cottage on the island for the few days left of his holiday. What a summer it has been, though too little rain, particularly out there by the sea.

4

And Anna?

Well, the children are in Dalarna with their grandmother. The doctor has prescribed fresh forest air after the infections of the spring term. But they are going to the summer place in the archipelago the second week in August. All three have recovered and are well. Henrik is away at a seminar.

Yes, Jacob knows that, an ecumenical seminar at the Sigtuna Foundation. Henrik is well. It has been a bad spring for us all with all that rampant illness. His insomnia is not so bad and he enjoys being by the sea. On her part, Anna is longing to see the children, but she doesn't want to leave Henrik on his own. He needs her presence.

And what is Anna doing in Stockholm? Jacob suddenly asks and she flushes, smiling at the same time. "I've been to the hairdresser's. A secret extravagance, you see. And last night I had dinner with the Hasselroths, nice people, my friends. I can never get Henrik to come with me. I don't really know why. But it's probably because they are friends of mine, not his. Tomorrow, I'm going up to Dalarna for a few days to stay with Mother and the children. Henrik will be alone for a week, but old Alma will be there to look after him, so that'll be all right. I want to be with Ma for a while, you see, Uncle Jacob. She's been so lonely since Ernst's death . . . and I . . ."

Anna turns her head away and runs her hand over her eyes, as if with impatience. "I can't quite be reconciled with my brother dying so suddenly and horribly like that. It's almost a year ago, but all the same. And Mamma loved him. I don't think she has ever loved anyone else."

She hides her face with her hand. Jacob sits still, listening carefully. Then he turns to face her and looks at her. She at once takes down her hand. There's so much, one great tangle. "I'm sorry, Uncle Jacob. I'm not the crying kind. But there's so much."

She collects herself and blows her nose in a large handkerchief. "I must go home. Henrik may well phone at four o'clock.

He starts worrying the moment I don't answer. If you'd like to come with me, I can give you a cup of coffee and something to eat." He nods and pats Anna's arm. "That'd be good. Much better than an early dinner before evensong. Come, let's go."

Anna's and Henrik's home is on the first floor of the parish block, a corner apartment looking out over the billowing greenery of the churchyard and a narrow side street. Everything in it is covered, rolled up or shrouded. The windows are slightly open to allow a thin cool draught through. The chandelier is shrouded in muslin, the extensive parquet floor bare, and all the furniture and other objects concealed under white and yellowing dust-sheets. But the grandfather clock in the corner is going and says a few minutes to four.

Anna has uncovered the blue velvet sofa and placed Uncle Jacob there, an elegant little table at his knee, on it the tea tray and open sandwiches, cheese, sausage and salt meat. She sits herself down in an armchair by the marble-topped drawing-room table, on the wall behind her a gilt-framed picture of the Virgin Mary and the Infant Jesus, an ageing Joseph expressing restrained surprise and some shepherds and angels just visible in the background. The picture is also covered with muslin.

Their quietly flowing conversation has ceased. Anna has turned to face the window, her hand moving over the marble surface. Jacob eats his sandwiches and lets the silence go on. "You don't mind if I smoke, do you," he says, as if in parenthesis, taking out his pipe and tobacco pouch. She smiles quickly, then at once turns serious.

Hand gesture.

"Have you time, Uncle Jacob?"

"I have evensong at six. Otherwise . . ."

"And after that?"

"All evening. As long as you like."

Silence.

"Perhaps this is wrong. I don't know."

"I've taken you through confirmation and I'm your spiritual adviser. You can say what you like. Or what you have to."

"Then I must."

Jacob leans forward and lights his pipe with elaborate care. Anna turns to him, the membranes of her eyes apparently about to burst. Then a deep breath. She looks at her hands resting on the arms of the chair.

"I'm an unfaithful wife.

"I live with another man.

"I'm deceiving Henrik.

"I'm full of anguish.

"Not guilty conscience or anything like that.

"That'd be silly.

"But anguish.

"I no longer know what to do.

"Another man.

"He's ten, well, eleven years younger.

"He's reading theology. Is to be a priest.

"But I can't break it off.

"I love him.

"For over a year.

"You know him, Uncle Jacob.

"It's Tomas.

"And then the children.

"And Henrik.

"Soon I won't be able to breathe."

Jacob nods. So she dares go on.

"Mamma was against my marriage to Henrik. When we finally married, she changed her attitude and decided to help us in every way. That took only two years. Two years."

She falls silent, smiling mournfully. Jacob says nothing.

"Yes, it took two years. Then I realised, of course, that my mother had been right. We did not suit each other. Henrik surrounded me on all sides with all his wounds. I was to be his mother and he would at last be allowed to be the child. My

7

child. My only child. He always had to know where I was. He had to know what I was thinking. It was like a prison, an emotional prison. I can't describe it in any other way."

Anna gets up and crosses the creaking floor with firm steps on her high heels, her clenched hands behind her back. It's important now not to give way to tears. Now she is to say just what the situation is. No, not what it is. She knows nothing about that. She is to say what occurs to her. She is to say how she just might possibly think things are. This mysterious fiction that has afflicted her reality and is threatening her life. (So badly? That must be something of an exaggeration? Presumably not. One day, like poisonous, dammed-up water, the pain must break through the dams and pour into her body, attacking her nerves, her mind, heart and loins. It will plunge her into lengthy torment and cause incurable damage to her body.)

"It was all so innocent and insidious. I had said to Tomas that he must come and see us during the summer. You know, don't you, Våroms is my parents' summer place, and it's in one of the most beautiful places in Dalarna. Henrik and I and the children were to spend the summer there. Mamma planned to be in the archipelago with her stepsons. I invited Tomas to come and stay over Midsummer. Henrik was going to be there, too, and Gertrud. Then Henrik couldn't come. He had to go to a conference. I thought of cancelling it, but Henrik thought Tomas should come anyhow. We joked and said that maybe Tomas and Gertrud would become a couple. The girl would make a very good wife for a priest. Well, Tomas came the day before Midsummer. Gertrud was already there by then. The maids were on holiday and I had a good girl from the village as help. I was feeling free and happy, everything glowing and flourishing. After raining for ages, the weather had changed and it was sunny every day. Well, yes, the way

I talk. I can hear myself saying all kinds of things you really think quite unimportant."

She is standing in front of Jacob, her hands still behind her back, looking at him. The tears well up, suddenly and unexpectedly. "We played with the children, we picked wild strawberries, we had ham with new potatoes and soured milk with ginger biscuits. In the evenings we played the piano and sang. Gertrud has such a lovely voice. And Tomas, yes. He knows such a lot of music. On other days we went for long outings over on the other side of the river, up to the outfield in Bäsna and Grånäs. We were always just us three together, Gertrud, Tomas and me. I was so pleased that . . . I was so pleased I had been able to . . . I was pleased, you see, Uncle Jacob. I was probably presumptuous, because I thought, I remember . . . I'm in love with this boy. I'm so in love that it's almost comical. I've no intention of being ashamed of falling in love. But I won't show it. I'll keep it to myself. Sometimes I left Tomas and Gertrud on their own. I didn't begrudge them each other. I actually *wanted* them to have each other. I, who had been so burdened, so weighed down, now I thought I could fly."

Anna makes a hasty gesture towards her hair, then sits down on the sofa beside Jacob and for a moment takes his great liver-spotted hand between hers, then gives it back.

"One of Tomas's last days at Våroms, I came down from my room to lay the table for dinner. The children were playing below the veranda and Gertrud was in the hammock, writing letters. Tomas helped me put out the glasses and plates. Then he stopped at the end of the table. I was over by the green cupboard and just about to take the plates out for dessert, and then he suddenly says he's fond of me. That he has been 'fond of me' – well, he said 'has loved me' for two years. That he couldn't understand what life would be like now he had to leave me. He also said that I mustn't be angry with him for saying it. Well, I don't actually know what he said. I sort of stopped listening. It was terrible and unreal and I thought briefly and clearly ... now everything'll go wrong. Now everything's spoilt. How could he be such an idiot?"

Jacob glances at the grandfather clock and with some difficulty gets up from the sofa.

"I must go now, my dear Anna. You'll have to excuse me, but I want to be at church in good time. If you feel like continuing our time together after evensong. I'll only be going home to take off my cassock and put on something more comfortable. Shall we say eight o'clock? Would that be all right?"

Anna thanks him rather faintly and he pats her arm. On his way out into the hall, he says suddenly: "You could come with me to church. They say we won't be many souls on a Sunday evening like this. It's true no one can hear what Arborelius is preaching and that might possibly be an advantage. But Ehrling plays the organ beautifully and the choir is to sing two of old Norén's motets. So there might be something for the soul after all."

He stands there thoughtfully for a while and then looks at her, almost sternly.

"If you'd like to take communion, then do so, Anna. If you're living in severe torment, if you're hard pressed, if you don't know what to do with yourself, it can be good to go to communion and be given permission to lay your distress on God's heart."

"I know nothing about God's heart, Uncle Jacob."

"You don't need to. But there's grace in the actual action. And perhaps that would relieve your suffering."

"I don't think I can."

"Do as you please. Anyhow, we'll see each other again at eight o'clock."

What does she do when she has been left alone? It is half past five on a Sunday evening. It is still warm, the sun glowing above the church cupola. Regrets? Relief? Sorrow? A dizziness that neither speaks nor replies. A hectic, penetrating anxiety.

Stop now. What am I doing? The anguish slips away and becomes flickering colours that evaporate and dissolve into floating shadows. She cannot distinguish Tomas's face, but she can see her mother quite clearly. Maybe she should phone Ma, who at this moment is sitting in the uncomfortable white chair by the window with its resplendent pelargoniums and view over the river, the heathlands and fading ridges. She is sure to be reading the Upsala paper, sitting there, small and erect, her glasses far down her nose, the sunlight coming diagonally through from the right, through the plants in the window boxes and shining on to her pale skin with laughter wrinkles round her eyes and the wrinkle of wisdom above the bridge of her nose. She has not been wearing her apron because it is Sunday, and her summer dress is of grey shantung with broad white cuffs and hemstitched collar. A grandchild is on the floor, Nils, aged five, playing quietly with building blocks and some dolls the size of a little finger.

What if she tried to get hold of Tomas instead? Just to find out what mood he is in, not tell him about confessions, nor to press him to say anything consoling or meaningful. But I probably can't get hold of him. He is lodging with an elderly relative and the telephone is on the wall in the hall, and he has also just had dinner at their shabby eating place with the two friends left of the bunch who usually eat together and are staying on for the summer in Upsala. And now he's sure to have gone to the Botanical Gardens to amble about down by the water-lily ponds, where it smells strongly of Chinese rose and still water. Or else he's sitting in the shade of the elms reading some book for his exams. She quickly thinks about his hand resting on the page and then she goes on thinking so that she is almost beside him. She stands with her head lowered, her finger to her lips as if requesting silence. No, not Tomas, not at the moment. Not later, either, perhaps never. Confession presumably entails something shattering and final. Anyhow something mysterious, which she does not dare include in her vision. There are short moments which muscle into life when she grasps the content, the exact content of her situation. Then she reaches out and grasps the back of a chair, and for a moment is utterly aware of the chill emanating from the sculptured white wood.

At the same far-reaching moment she sees herself as an image – an image of Anna and Tomas. They are naked and sweaty. She is lying on her back in his arms with both hands round his head, pressing his forehead to her. She parts her legs and opens, pressing her back against the coarse bedspread. Dusk has fallen in the bare room, the glowing embers of the fire rustling in the tiled stove, listless snowflakes outlined against the dark branches in the park. The moment beyond fear. The moment is as unfathomable as death. Now, at this moment, as she touches the sculptured back of the chair, she realises, indeed she feels with the essence of her emotions the sharpness of sensations, the twilight, the confusion of sweaty bodies, the smell of stale tobacco smoke, the rough surface of the bedspread, the untamed moment still trembling in her nerves. The frightened, expressionless face of the boy, his eyes closed and lips pressed together. He whimpers slightly. He turns his head aside, his hand resting against her long hair flowing over the stiffly soiled pillow with its sharp hemstitching. In that brief moment, her emotions and reason grasp the irretrievable cruelty of their meeting of love. And now, at this moment, she sees quite clearly that she has no regrets. She blames no one, neither herself nor anyone else. She involves neither God nor faith in her dark confusion. She realises she will never go deeper down into herself than now. She is falling headlong into innermost spaces, a raging light that dazzles and banishes the gentle twilight. Anna often liked saying she wanted to see the truth. She imagined she longed for the truth, that she desired it; it became like an infatuation. Perhaps it would be like seeing the face of God. She herself liked to appoint herself an apostle of the truth. With words of that

12

kind she gained particular respect. For brief moments she regretted her clever corrections. She whispered silently to herself: what kind of truth am I talking about? And then she was slightly ashamed (but not much) of her fleeting insight.

The clock strikes six and the summoning bell clangs over sun-emptied streets. Anna pulls herself together; the overwhelming moment has evaporated. She turns again into the room, thus leaving the chair. "Now then, Anna," she says out aloud to herself. "You're not to phone Ma, nor Tomas. But you might as well make your way down to church and listen to the music. That'll do you good."

She takes the lovely summer hat off the hat rack and looks at herself in the dim hall mirror. She examines herself with the cool objectivity of an actress. In her undeniable despair, this provides a brief but intense enjoyment. She thrusts her arms into the jacket sleeves and straightens out the lacy patterns at the top of her blouse. Gloves, handbag, prayer book. And goes. Down the stairs, across the street on to the stone-laid path of the churchyard, rapid steps towards the great doorway. The prelude to the first hymn is being intoned, few souls in the green pews. The sunlight is hurling horizontal spears through the huge dark-blue cupola with its constellations. The church is cold after the fragrant warmth of the churchyard. It smells of mouldy cellar, dead flowers and old timber. The altar candles flicker uncertainly beneath the high picture of the cross: the dress of the Holy Mother glows dimly red in the horrible scenery. The weeping sinner is clutching at the foot of the cross, the thunder clouds darkening behind the still illuminated Jerusalem.

Anna sinks down into the pew and smiles weakly at Mrs Arborelius sitting by the aisle beside a large red-haired daughter in a sailor suit, a sailor hat on her straggly curls.

The service flows on in its practised way. The Reverend Arborelius speaks, his deep bass voice thundering in the arch of the temple and bouncing off the tombs in the stone floor.

The choir sings the mildly harsh motets, both from the Psalms. "Lead me in the way everlasting" and "And call upon me in the day of trouble: I will deliver thee, and thou shalt glorify me."

The spacious and well-equipped kitchen faces the courtyard and its elms, transverse walls and storage sheds. A faded red summer curtain billows at the open window. The larder is so large it holds an old-fashioned refrigerator, still in use. Along the wall is a partly folding kitchen table with blue-painted wooden chairs round it, shelves on the walls full of copper pans and disparate ornamental objects. The work tops by the sink are of marble, long and low, spacious cupboards under-neath them. In the corner next to the protruding flue is a sturdy ingenious 1909 wood-stove containing two baking ovens and a gleaming copper hot water tank. The stove-rings are numerous and the openings above the fire four in number. Beside and at right angles to the wood-stove is a two-burner gas-stove. The floor is covered with linoleum, newly varnished for the summer, only partly covered by home-woven rag-rugs. Two shoemaker's lamps hang high up in the ceiling, when in use throwing out a pleasing yellow light. A short flight of stairs in the wall opposite the window goes down into a maid's room.

Smells of summer come from the courtyard and of varnish from the linoleum.

The parish priest is sitting on a wooden chair at the kitchen table, filling his pipe. It is eight o'clock and still light, the sun just reaching the roof and chimneys of the apartment house opposite. A gramophone is being played by an open window. Otherwise it is all quite still.

Jacob fills his pipe from his tobacco pouch. The tip of his forefinger is yellow with nicotine and scarred from small burns. He has taken off his clerical garb and put on crumpled grey flannel trousers and a long hand-knitted cardigan. His dog-collar has been replaced by something more comfortable round his neck. The neatly tied tie is dark blue. His waistcoat is slightly shabby and has a button missing, the cuffs round strong hairy wrists sticking out of the cardigan sleeves.

The reason why Jacob is sitting in the kitchen is the modest supper Anna has improvised – onion and tomato omelette, small sausages and new potatoes. She pours out a glass of schnapps for both of them and they also share a bottle of chilled pilsner. Jacob praises her swift initiative and drinks her health. She is standing beside him at the table.

So in this way, the tragedy pauses. Jacob and Anna allow themselves to eat, only making small talk.

Anna has taken off her apron. After she has poured out the coffee, she has sat down on the stool by the sink, facing the window. Jacob stirs his coffee, takes three lumps of sugar, hesitates, then takes a fourth.

"Most people think Luther abolished confession. But he didn't. He prescribed what he called 'private conversation'. But he didn't know much about human beings, that splendid reformer. Face to face in broad daylight is difficult. So it's better done in the semi-darkness of the confessional, the mumbling voices, in the smell of incense."

Jacob looks at his quietly reeking pipe and smiles thoughtfully. "I can no longer see you," he says then. "The evening light from the window obliterates your face. If you like, Anna dear, we can go on talking. If not, we can just go on sitting here together, feeling affection. That's also very purposeful."

But Anna really does want to talk.

"My childhood was incredibly harmonious – and fun. I sometimes wonder whether that was so entirely useful. Maybe you're given wrong ideas. And I've probably been naive. Only in that I married Henrik. I could see how damaged he was, but in my boundless self-confidence, I thought I was destined to save him. Can you imagine anything stupider? Mamma warned me. Warned me and tried to stop me, but I was stubborn. Of course I loved him in a childish and arrogant way. But I knew nothing. Neither about him, nor about myself.

In two years, Uncle Jacob, in two short years, we'd thrown away our capital of love. One night I ran away from Forsboda to Upsala. I got there early in the morning and wept and begged my mother to help me. She was attentive and kindly, but unyielding. The next morning I was made to take the train back to my marriage. It was insane."

Anna laughs joylessly and turns to the window, the sunlight gone now, a reddish light colouring the dirty yellow façades. Under the great trees, two small boys are busy with a rickety bicycle. A tall woman in a crumpled greyish-blue dress opens a window and leans out. Other female figures can just be seen inside the apartment, chat and laughter and careless piano music pouring out over the courtyard.

"No," says Anna, suddenly and decisively. "I couldn't do what you recommend, Uncle Jacob. I did want to go to communion, but I stopped myself."

They have left the kitchen: "No, no, I'll clear away later. Let's go into the library so that you can sit in a comfortable armchair and smoke your evening cigar. Henrik has been given a whole box by Gustavsson, a business man . . . in gratitude for something, I don't know what, though I think because Henrik went to see his old mother at the Erika Foundation."

She takes Jacob's arm and they walk through the darkening rooms, where the shrouded furniture glows like arctic formations. The library is a square room with two windows facing the churchyard and Storgatan, the walls lined with bookcases. A small home altar is set into the wall between the bookcases, on it the open family bible. Above the bible is a half-metre wooden crucifix portraying "the triumphant saviour". An oil painting, dark and Dutch, hangs above the big leather sofa, an ingenious chamber organ at right angles to the sofa, and there are comfortable low leather armchairs below the window. A massive library table extends along the middle of the floor.

"Henrik hardly ever smokes cigars, but he maintains these are excellent."

Anna has opened the silver cigar box and taken out a cigar. She puts it to her ear and rolls it back and forth, then nods approvingly.

"Pappa was an enthusiastic cigar-smoker. Fine cigars and fine railway engines were his passions (possibly Mamma, too, but that is less certain). I loved sitting on his lap when he was smoking. So he taught me very early on to treat cigars with care and respect."

She opens up a gilded knife with an ivory handle and snips the chosen cigar, then hands it to Jacob, lights a long match and holds it out for him. There is a moment of violent puffing. Then Jacob looks at his cigar with appreciation.

Anna leans against the high wooden armchair at the library table, her arms resting on the back as she looks out of the window.

"It was like this, if you want to hear, Uncle Jacob. Tomas and I were alone in his wretched lodgings. It was an icy cold January day, dusk already falling. I had told him I had to go back to Stockholm and it would be a long time before we could meet again. He stood quite still, his hands on my shoulders. I had already put my coat on. I was leaving. It was at that moment I chose."

"You chose?" (emphasis on both words)

"I took off my coat. I took off my dress. I sat down on a chair and took off my winter boots and my petticoat and bodice and stockings. I took out my hairpins. In the end I was sitting there on the chair in nothing but my shift. I hadn't looked at Tomas all the time I'd been undressing. Then I looked at him. He was standing over by his work table. Then he shook his head and said no, no, no, not this. He was that precise, Uncle Jacob. But I no longer had any choice. For me, there was no possibility of turning back. Yes, I know it sounds dramatic, but I can't find any other words for it. So I took his hand and pulled him towards me, he fell to his knees and I had his head in my hands and his forehead against my breast.

That's what it was like. Does it upset you that I tell you all these details, Uncle Jacob?"

"You must decide that for yourself."

"I took him to me, you see, Uncle Jacob. And then I had to console him."

She suddenly laughs and strikes the back of the chair with her clenched fist.

"He was inconsolable. He assured me that he had betrayed me and Henrik, who was his best friend. He thought he had been weak and behaved appallingly. He said that God would never forgive him this. He was like a terrified child. Then we started kissing again and he was as eager as I was. Nothing . . . nothing. No. Nothing."

She runs her hand across her forehead as if there had been a cobweb there to wipe away.

"I have thought about regrets. But I have no regrets. I have thought about sin, but that just becomes a word. I have put prohibitions like a high wall between him and me. But at the very slightest chance of seeing him, I at once knock down that wall. I think about Henrik, but Henrik's face is unclear. I hear what he says . . . I mean, I hear his voice. But he's not really real. I think that I ought to . . . I know that I ought to . . . no, that's probably not true. And the children. I have become kinder towards Henrik, too. Things have been better between us . . . things are better in every way. I can be tender and loving towards him and he is pleased and not so irritable and anguished. Everything has become better since I gave myself permission to love Tomas. He is also at peace and no longer has his attacks of 'awareness of sin', as he calls it. We can't see each other all that often, but whenever I am in Upsala to see my mother, we meet."

She has talked a great deal and for a long time. No anguish. No regrets or shyness. She stands by the chair with her arms on the back, looking out into the summer dusk over the dark treetops in the churchyard.

"If everything is as marvellous as you've just told me, why did you start crying?"

"You caught me out, Uncle Jacob. I had just been with Tomas in a room in a boarding house, almost all afternoon. I went to the train with Henrik. Then I went straight to Tomas. We hadn't seen each other for over a month . . . six weeks, I think. It was so upsetting . . . no, not sorrowful, but upsetting. I didn't see you sitting there in the shade. And then you called out and I was so comically frightened, as if caught out . . . yes, caught out. And as we sat there talking so pleasantly, I had a feeling . . ."

Silence. Yet another silence. Anna is shaping words that are not spoken.

"I think I can guess what you were feeling."

"Of course you can't!" says Anna in annoyance. "If I'm to be honest, I was frightened."

"Frightened of me?"

"It was like a pillar, black and gleaming, reaching right up to the sky. It was a momentary feeling that passed in a second. Then we were sitting there talking. And it was just pleasant, not in the least peculiar."

"Then you started crying."

"Yes. You see, I realised all that joy was to be taken from me, leaving room for so much suffering and . . . unfathomable misery. It was a brief insight . . . just like that pillar, and it had gone in a few seconds and I heard my own voice telling you about . . . then . . . then the tears came. And I couldn't . . ."

"You could've blamed anything."

"I was looking at your big hand, Uncle Jacob. And I thought if God has a hand, which I don't believe, but if God has a hand then it looks like yours. Then I thought about the hymn: last my Lord I thee pray, take my hand in thine so thou . . ."

For a brief moment she is overwhelmed by a rush of pain. She goes round the library table and sits down on the uncomfortable monk's chair at the organ. Nothing is said for quite a long time, which is noted to assist anyone interested in the way a conversation of this kind moves and breathes.

"From all that you've just told me, I can understand that you *really* did want to communicate with me, although you thought you couldn't."

"Yes, I suppose that's it," says Anna in a distinct voice of a little girl. "Isn't that always so? A very great joy, a joy so great it's unfathomable . . . in its turn it summons up every kind of darkness, every possible torment and terror.

"I was made to taste the pain waiting behind the joy, I suppose. If it's *not* God who has given me Tomas, then I'm a long way from God and that's good. I know you're thinking I'm being unacceptably blasphemous."

"It's not for you to decide what I think! I remember when you came to confirmation classes. You'd always done your homework and when we had our discussions, you brought up pertinent questions. I also saw you were a friend to your class-mates. I knew you came from a loving home. I knew both your mother and your father, your mother best of all. I probably wondered what kind of life lay ahead of you."

Jacob leans forward, grasping the dying cigar between his thumb and forefinger. He lights it, puffs out smoke, the aroma spreading in the twilight. Anna bows her head and looks at her open palm . . . then she makes a little gesture of restrained impatience.

"All that kindly security. Even at school . . . I mean the nursing school. I saw all that misery – especially the children. But that didn't touch my security. And all those years with Henrik – twelve years – difficult and hardworking years, not at all as I had imagined. But the security was there. Mamma and Pappa. My brother. Trädgårdsgatan. Everything was there all the time. I lived a long way inside that security."

Silence. Yet another silence.

"Do you want me to go, Anna?"

"No. I'd like you to stay a little while longer. But I don't think I've anything more to say."

"And Anna, why have you told me, *really?*"

"If I dare think about it . . .

"If I just think about the smallest thing of all.

"Then I see that we are living under threat.

"That I'm becoming more and more restricted.

"The children and Henrik and Tomas and I . . .

"We are moving close to a catastrophe.

"A life-catastrophe.

"Either I do nothing at all, but then I can . . . no, that's impossible. Is there really any way out? And the next question . . . and it frightens me most of all . . . do I really *want* a way out? Then I at once think about the children. And it's so difficult, I push those thoughts away, yes, they're as good as unendurable. Now I'm crying a little and that's not just selfishness, but it hurts damnably. Say what you like about Henrik, but he's good to the children. Maybe too strict, especially with the boys, but he's loving and tender-hearted with them . . . then I would be taking the children from him. That'd be unjust. No, it's a timed infernal machine, ticking away, and sometimes I can hear it very clearly. And I am frightened . . . at the same time I'm filled with longing."

She suddenly looks Jacob straight in the eye and smiles almost cheerfully. "So *that's* it, Uncle Jacob. I haven't told a single person about all this. I think a few have some idea, Gertrud perhaps. She's seen Tomas and me together, and Märta. She took me aside one day and warned me about one thing and another. We never spelt it out. Märta's on the other side of the world now, a missionary and doctor. Gertrud was probably just as much in love with Tomas, but she's never said anything. So now you know, Uncle Jacob. I don't really know what I'd hoped for. Maybe that you'd give me some good advice, a solution. Or forgiveness of my sins."

Jacob smokes his cigar. It's almost finished. He observes the glow flickering inside the thin tobacco leaf.

"If you want my compassion, I can tell you that it lies deep down. If you want my absolution, then you may not have it, as I don't think you feel any regret whatsoever. If, on the other hand, you want my advice, I could say one or two things, presuming that you'll take me seriously. With that I mean you should follow my instructions. But you have to believe that I am speaking to you from the best of my judgement."

"I understand."

"Everything I'm going to say to you will make you rebel. You'll be miserable and angry and rebellious."

"Maybe I'll be grateful."

"I doubt it. First of all – you must, unconditionally, break off all liaison with your friend. Even if you yourself are experiencing profound and rich emotional satisfaction, you must put an end to the relationship. Tomas is committing a great crime. It could damage him for life. If his lapse also becomes known, his future will become even further jeopardised, not to say made impossible. You say you love him, and I believe you. To be loved by a person like you is a priceless gift. I mean, I have *not* said you should stop loving him, which would be a strange demand. What I'm telling you is that you are to cut off all connections, and I mean *all*. In that way, you would show him your love."

Anna is looking steady at him. The street lights have now gone on and are casting reflections on the ceiling, so they can distinguish each other's features. Jacob is perhaps waiting for Anna to say something, but she stays silent.

"You must also tell Henrik everything."

"I can't do that."

"You must."

"No, no, I can't. Anything, but not tell him."

"You must."

"What purpose would that serve? No, that's impossible."

"The truth, Anna! You're entangled in a skein of lies. The

22

longer you live in that tangle, the more wretched your life will be."

"Uncle Jacob! Henrik is a person who can scarcely cope with the strains everyday life puts in his way. He is weak and full of anxieties. His workload is immense. The truth would crush him. We have a fairly bad marriage, wretched in many ways, both spiritually and physically. But we have a kind of considerate comradeship which binds us together. And it has helped us through twelve years. Comradeship and the children. If I drag in the truth, all hell would descend on us. No, Uncle Jacob, no, no."

"Don't you see, your suppression of the truth is profoundly selfish. There is, I have to tell you, a possibility that through the truth, Henrik might mature to a better life."

"A better life! Forgive me, but Henrik is not that sort of person. He evades whenever he can evade things. He runs away whenever there is a chance to run away. If he is for one single moment at a loss, he becomes furiously angry or ill. He'd go under. *That's* the truth. I know he's a good priest. He's a conscientious spiritual adviser and has helped a great many people. But inside all that, he is a lamentable terrified wretch. I *can't* tell the truth. Do you *know* what things are like for us? I mean what I called our intimate life? Sometimes I want to howl with disgust and humiliation. But it's possible to live from day to day and that's the main thing. I can't tell Henrik about my physical life. I can't even work out how he would react . . . he would perhaps . . . And the guilt . . . that guilt . . ."

"You must understand that I understand. Nonetheless, the *truth* is the only possibility. You must forestall a humiliating disclosure."

"And who will help me when all hell breaks loose? Will I be able to turn to God? Or perhaps even you, Uncle Jacob? Or to my mother? What do I say if Henrik throws me out on to the street? Shall I go to Tomas (laughs slightly) and say that now, you poor thing, now you'll have to look after me and my children? No! I will never tell the truth you're demanding. I don't believe in that sort of honesty. I purchase my daily life with lies and betrayal. It's worth it. I shall bear my guilt all by myself and I have no intention of asking anyone for help. Neither God nor you, Uncle Jacob."

"You talk of guilt as if you had a grasp of what *real* guilt entails. You don't know that. It's possible my words hurt and wound you. It's possible that you'll have to expose yourself and yours to trials. But if you have chosen the truth, you will become strong."

Anna smiles inwardly. "Yes," she says. "Yes, yes. Naturally. If you go the way of truth you become strong. If you choose the truth you solve insoluble problems."

"I must go now, Anna. I understand why you distance yourself. Nor do I demand that you should think as I do. I can't even remember whether you asked my advice. I have simply said what occurred to me."

"Is it so strange that I defend myself?"

"Be angry, by all means. After all, I'm talking to you from my well-ordered reality. My own crises and shortcomings are scarcely relevant at this particular moment. So be angry, please do. But think about it. You are a wise young person. I imagine that what I have said has existed in your mind for quite a long time. As clear realities."

"And so I know . . ."

"Abandon for a moment your preconceived idea of Henrik's possibilities."

"Thank you for your solicitude, Uncle Jacob."

"I shall include you in my evening prayers."

She lowers her head. They stop and stand still in the spacious hall, his hand on the door-handle.

"Turn on the light so that I can see your face."

She turns the switch. A sleepy pair of lights go on in the brass brackets each side of the door.

"Look me in the eye. So. You're angry."

"No."

"Yes, you are. You're angry and disappointed. But what did you expect?"

"I don't know. I just wanted . . ."

"We act out many rôles. Some because it's fun, some because others want us to act out those rôles. Mostly because we want to protect ourselves."

"Yes, I think so."

"Then I imperceptibly lose what is *not* a rôle. When I keep on living, I get away from what is . . . 'myself' or whatever it's called."

"Then I can at once say that now, at this very moment, I am *at last* 'me'. Life with Henrik took me further and further into what you call 'rôles'."

She looks anxiously, pleadingly at Jacob. He doesn't meet her gaze, but instead gives her cheek a quick caress and shakes his head.

"I remember what you said that evening before your confirmation. 'I pray to God that I shall be of use. I'm tremendously strong.' Do you remember?"

"Yes, I do. I know. It was childish. But I *was* childish, after all."

"God has heard your prayer now."

"No."

"Don't you believe God concerns himself with your misery?"

"No."

"Don't you believe any longer?"

"No."

"Don't you say your prayers?"

"No."

"What does Tomas say?"

"He says that my 'turning away', as he calls it, frightens him. Do you believe in God, Uncle Jacob? A Father in Heaven? A God of Love? A God with hands and heart and watchful eyes?"

25

"All that's unimportant to me."

"Unimportant? How can the form of God be unimportant?"

"Don't say that word 'God'. Say 'The Holy One'. The Sanctity of Man. Everything else is attribute, disguise, manifestations, tricks, desperations, ritual, cries of despair in the darkness and the silence. You can never calculate or capture the Sanctity of Man. At the same time, it's something to hold on to, something quite concrete. Unto Death. What happens thereafter is hidden. But one thing is sure ... we are surrounded by events we do not grasp with our senses, but which constantly influence us. Only the Poets, Musicians and Saints have given us mirrors of the Unfathomable. They have seen, known, understood. Not wholly, but in fragments. It is consoling to me to think about the Sanctity of Man and the mysterious Immensities surrounding us. What I am saying to you now is not a metaphor, for it is reality. Inscribed in the Sanctity of Man is the Truth. No one can commit violence against the Truth without going wrong. Without doing harm."

They have sat down on chairs beside the hall door. The lights from the wall brackets officiate sleepily. It is dark beyond the open window of the dining-room. A lone song-thrush concealed in the foliage heralds the as yet invisible dawn.

Second Conversation
August 1925

A month has gone by. It is August, the weather mild, half past eight in the evening, Henrik sitting on the steamer jetty. The clouds are low and it drizzles occasionally, the twilight grey and shadowless. It is still summer.

He is alone on the jetty, smoking a cigarillo more to keep off the midges than for enjoyment. He is bareheaded, his light brown hair thinning out over his high forehead. His eyes are blue and friendly, his moustache well trimmed. Under his raincoat, he has on a summer jacket and flannel trousers, collar and tie.

Then he sees the boat across the bay over by the Stendörren jetty. It backs and turns to head for Smådalarö, approaching the island at good speed. The gangway is thrown out with a loud thump. Anna is already standing in the bows. She picks up her luggage and hurries ashore. The gangway is immediately drawn back, a bell clangs in the interior of the hull and the propeller whisks up the dark transparent water. The boat backs, gets up speed and disappears beyond Rödudd point, lights on in some of the cabins' round portholes.

Henrik takes Anna's case and the basket of paper bags and packages, at the same time kissing her on the mouth. She stands on tiptoe and kisses his cheek. He has shaved for their meeting.

The moment has now come when from my position here at my desk on Fårö island on June 18th, 1992, I am to approach these two people struggling up the steep stony slope from the

Smådalarö jetty one August evening in 1925. Anyhow, I am making an attempt. I don't really know why I am making all this effort. I don't know, but none the less, I am, and approaching with whirlwind soundless speed. I can see them.

The summer place was built at the turn of the century and is ten minutes' walk from the jetty. The rear veranda faces the evening sun and the narrow gravel path. The house is yellow with white corners and has four rooms and a cramped old-fashioned kitchen. The dining-room faces a green slope, the bay and Pannholmen isle. There are two smaller rooms on the upper floor, one facing north, the other south, the idyll completed by a green-painted privy perched on a smooth rock. At the end of the house is an oak many hundreds of years old, huge, healthy and leafy. That is why the house is called Ekebo, the home of the oak.

They struggle up the slope from the jetty, the path stony and uneven. The pines are high and still, and it's drizzling. "How stupid of me not to bring an umbrella," says Henrik apologetically, putting down the case and panting. Anna takes a few steps past him, stops and turns round. "The sun was out in town, of course, so I didn't think of taking an umbrella. Here, let me help. We can take the case between us."

They lug it together, but as Anna is so much smaller than Henrik, it is troublesome.

"Actually, it's better if I carry it alone," says Henrik.

"Then I'll take the basket."

"No, I want that to balance the other side."

"Oh well, then, I don't know."

Anna laughs and pulls off her hat. The rain trickles on to her face and her thick dark-brown hair. She is wearing a dark-blue summer coat, grey skirt and a silk blouse with small buttons.

"The rain's nice," she says, wiping her forehead and cheek with the back of her hand.

"We've not had a drop here for three weeks. Well, you know that. I imagine it was just as dry up in Dalarna?"

28

"We were worried the well might dry up. But at least we have the river."

"Actually, we've been terribly economic with the water. We only use it for cooking and fruit drinks. We wash in the sea."

"Apropos washing, the boys send their love, and Lillan, too, of course. Mamma and I agreed to give the boys free rein. They disappear after breakfast and spend all day with their friends in the village. They don't appear until dinner time, and as I said, we don't fuss about times and cleanliness. Washing ears and cutting nails are done on Saturdays. They are all well. Lillan cut her bottom slightly on a broken potty. It bled quite a bit and the boys have grazes here and there, but that's all part of it."

Anna chats on, helping with the basket a little. She chats on and Henrik happily listens.

"And how is Tante Karin?"

"Oh, Mamma!"

Anna stops at the top of the slope and Henrik puts the case down, and the basket, which is heavy with the bags and packages from Gustavsson's Grocery Store.

"Well, Mamma, yes. And Ebba. It's just three months since Ernst died. Mamma grieves, I can see that, and Ebba's eyes are swollen with weeping. Sometimes at night I could hear her whimpering. But both of them are calm and cheerful. Little Jan is three now, yes, you know that. We had a fine birthday, I'll have you know. I find it difficult to make contact with Ebba. We try, both of us, but we don't get through to each other. Her grief and my grief seem to be incomparable, if you see what I mean. Big brother Ernst. It's impossible to take in."

Anna gestures with her hand and starts walking. Henrik follows a few steps behind.

"And when are Lillan and the boys coming? Have you decided anything?"

"Mamma's going to Stockholm at the end of next week and she'll take the children with her. Then we can celebrate

Lillan's birthday out here before we have to move back into town."

"So we haven't many days together."

"We agreed to move back in on the fifth of September."

"Yes, yes. Fifth of September, a Tuesday."

"You agreed to that, too."

"Yes, yes. I know that."

"We'll be together for almost three weeks. That's fairly good, anyhow, isn't it, Henrik?"

"I'm preaching in Hedvig on the first of September."

"You have healthy, sunburnt, happy children. Remember what Dr Fürstenberg said in the spring. The children must have forest air."

"Yes, yes, of course."

"We have to be grateful to Ma for looking after them all summer, despite her grief. And all her troubles."

"Yes, yes, of course. Of course."

"We must be grateful."

"I *am* grateful."

They meet Professor Ruthström and his wife Adelaide out for an evening walk, their dark wooden house looming up across the road from Ekebo. The professor is Professor of Violin at the Academy of Music, more of a virtuoso than a teacher. He is small and fat and well-groomed, his unruly hair grey and reddish. Mrs Adelaide is also small, fat and red-haired. She comes from Mecklenburg and was once a leading dramatic soprano. Both have fair skins and liver-spots on their faces, their large heads squat on their shoulders.

The Pastor and the Professor couples greet each other courteously and enquire in proper order after each other's state of health. Mrs Adelaide wishes to know when the boys are coming home from Dalarna and Mrs Anna tells her that will be happening the following week and that Dag is looking forward to going sailing with Siegfrid. The Professor puts down his umbrella and says the rain has definitely stopped before it had begun and the Pastor replies that he had heard thunder in the distance and possibly seen some lightning out over the bay. Then they wish each other good evening and continue in each direction. Henrik says that Professor Ruthström is to play Glazunov's violin concerto at the beginning of the season and his wife had already promised them free tickets. He adds that he practises for four hours every day – with the window open, too, and that that is a bit of a strain. "They are such nice pleasant people," says Anna. "If only they weren't so political. All that endless preaching about the greatness of Germany and her downfall. Sometimes it's quite mad."

Then they are home and go into the hall through the open veranda. Anna takes off her coat and throws her hat on to the shelf. Henrik puts the case in Anna's room, which is connected with Henrik's bed-cum-workroom by a narrow sliding door.

"I think I'll go down to the jetty and take a dip."

"I'll come with you to make sure you don't drown."

"Wait, I'll be with you in a moment," says Anna, pushing Henrik out.

After he has lit the oil lamp on the sideboard in the dining-room, Henrik goes out on to the glassed-in veranda. He is suddenly uneasy, almost anxious. He sits down on one of the creaking basket chairs.

Anna walks quickly through the dining-room. "I wonder whether we should leave that lamp on. In that case, we must shut the window, otherwise the midges and other insects will get in." She has put on a black bathing costume and a shabby dark-red dressing-gown. "Let's go then," she says, smiling quickly. She kicks off her sandals, picks them up and runs barefoot down towards the smooth, gleaming dark waters of the bay. Henrik puts his hands behind his back and follows slowly.

Anna throws herself headlong into the water. She has tied a scarf round her hair, but it comes loose at once and trails in the water. "It's really warm," she calls. Henrik has sat down on an upturned box. Anna swims towards the jetty and hauls herself out.

She quickly covers herself in the voluminous dressing gown, and turning away, she pulls off her wet bathing costume. Then she sits down on Henrik's box and dries her feet on a coarse towel and pulls on her sandals. She throws her wet hair back over her shoulders, running her hands through the thick, dully gleaming strands. "Come on, Henrik, a cup of tea and a bite to eat would be good now," she says, and takes his hand.

He takes hold of her by the hips, hard, and pulls her to him, pressing his forehead against her stomach. He moves his head to and fro, opening the loosely tied dressing gown. He kisses her stomach and her hip, all the time holding firmly on to her. She frees herself – not violently, but slowly and firmly. He gets up and embraces her. He kisses her damp face, her throat and mouth. "No, not like that," she says quietly. "Don't hold on to me like that. Come on, let's go up to the kitchen and have some tea. I'm actually getting rather cold. Come on, Henrik," she says gently, holding out her hand.

It may well be nearing eleven o'clock at night and the rain has started again, quietly and steadily. Anna is in her long-sleeved, pale-blue flannel nightgown and has swept a rug round her stomach and legs, her white bedsocks on her feet. She drinks her tea, slowly. Henrik is sitting at the other end of the table. He has taken a glass of pilsner to keep her company. There is an old oil lamp on the table, hissing faintly and smoking slightly. Husband and wife have ceased speaking.

Then Henrik gets up decisively, takes a step towards Anna and stands in front of her.

"It's been four weeks. I've missed you. I've missed the children, too, but most of all you. I haven't complained. It'd be shameful and spoilt of me to whine, when things are so good for me. Oh, yes, I've been well looked after. And I haven't been alone, either. Gertrud has been here and Per Hasselroth and

Einar and his fiancée and a lot of other nice people. So I don't mean to complain. That would be both ungrateful and spoilt of me. And you've written such tender and loving letters. Your letters have been a great help. I've read them in the evenings, when I've gone to bed. And we've spoken on the telephone, though that's double-edged, it's so impersonal. Though it's been lovely to hear your voice. And now you're here at last. I've been counting the days and worried something might happen to stop you from coming. Now you are here, anyhow. And best of all . . . we can be on our own for a few days."

Anna's forefinger is tracing a pattern on the tablecloth. "But I don't want to tonight," she says quickly and quietly.

Henrik stays where he is and says nothing.

"Anna?"

"No, Henrik. No."

"What is it?"

"I don't think it's anything at all. It's just that I want to be left in peace."

"Haven't you been left in peace enough?"

"I must get used to it. You mustn't stand like that making demands."

"What peculiar words. I'm demanding nothing."

"But I don't want to."

She shakes her head, gets up and takes her cup to the sink. Henrik embraces her hard and presses her against him. The cup falls to the floor and breaks. She turns rigid with disinclination and anger, then frees herself, but no longer gently and apologetically. For a moment she turns to him as if wanting to say something, pale and out of breath. Henrik is more astonished and frightened.

"Have I done something wrong? What is it, Anna? Surely you can . . ."

But Anna goes, stopping for a moment in the hall as if about to go out into the rain, but remembers her clothing and instead hurries into her room as if pursued. She shuts the door and turns the key. Locks.

Henrik is bewildered, uneasy and finally angry, surly and embittered. The soft desire in the crannies of his body runs out and at first leaves a vacuum, then suddenly there is prickly, tearful anger. He goes out on to the veranda and gazes into the rustling sighing darkness. The lamp on the dining-room sideboard shines on the window pane and his dark reflection. Fear, anger, heaviness of heart.

Fairly soon, fear takes over. He wants to challenge it, hurries into his room and knocks on the narrow sliding door. "Anna, forgive me for being stupid and clumsy. Anna. Answer me, Anna dear, I *beg* you."

Anna is walking soundlessly across the floor. To and fro. Following the edge of the rag-rug, her head forward, her arms folded across her breast, her head lowered, following the dark parallel lines of the floorboards. She is breathing deeply as if from lack of oxygen, as if she were at a tremendous height where the air is thin and the sky dark. She stops and kicks off her meek slippers, stands still – listening to Henrik's low-voiced pleading on the other side of the sliding door. Now and again the gleaming brass door-handle moves, but cautiously, timidly.

Then he shouts and gives the door a kick. Fear and rage. Strikes with his clenched fist. "You may not treat me like this! Anna! At least answer me."

Silence. Anna stands without moving, head down, the long dark hair falling forward over her cheeks.

Then Henrik: "Anna!" His voice is calm now. "We must speak to each other. I refuse to give in. I'll sit out on the veranda and wait for you. I intend to go on waiting. Go on waiting, Anna. Do you hear what I'm saying? I want you to come out and explain what's wrong."

He lets go the door-handle and goes away. She hears him rummaging about on the veranda, pulling a chair along the floor, sitting down and lighting his pipe.

All this she can hear as she stands quite still in the middle of the black-and-blue striped rag-rug.

It is true people often talk about "decisive moments". Dramatists in particular make much of this fiction. The truth is probably that such moments hardly exist, but it just looks as if they do. "Decisive moments" and "fateful decisions" . . . they sound plausible. But if looked at carefully, the moment is not at all decisive: for a long time, emotions and thoughts have consciously or unconsciously been flowing in the same direction. The actual breakthrough is a fact far back in the past, far back in obscurity.

Anna starts moving. In her darkness, her anger and her suffocation, she is inexorably on her way to alter the lives of a great many people. At this moment of the breakthrough, real reality, a sense of mysterious desire is moving on the edge of her consciousness. Everything will collapse now. In this way I shall be annihilated. So it is *at last* at an end. She unlocks her door, goes through the dining-room, picking up the lamp on the way and once out on the veranda puts it carefully down on the circular basketry table by the wall. She turns up the wick. Like that, she and Henrik can now look into each other's faces. Henrik attempts an apology. "Forgive me. I behaved like a child, but I was actually frightened. I know we've had rows before, quite often, too, but locked doors have not been part of our behaviour."

Anna has pulled up a chair and sat down opposite Henrik on a small white-painted basket chair, old and slightly shabby, its arms sloping.

"I've got something to tell you that will hurt."

"Now I'm really worried." He smiles appealingly.

"The fact is that for quite a time I've been living with another man."

"Don't say it . . ."

"Whom I love . . . "

"Whom you love . . ."

"Whom I love more than any other human being. I live with him in every way – with my body and all my senses and in my heart."

" . . . truth?"

"This is the truth, Henrik. I have hesitated, I mean I haven't known whether I should tell you. But this evening when you made demands on me, I couldn't go on dissembling. Tomas and I have been together all day. I came from him."

"Tomas?"

"I don't want to any longer. I can't."

"Tomas?"

"You know him."

"Tomas Egerman."

"Yes. Tomas Egerman."

"He's a . . . but he's reading . . ."

"He's reading for his exams in Upsala. He'll be qualified in roughly two years. Two and a half."

"He was there at the parish evening and sang the Schumann romances."

"Yes, he was originally a musician. He's taken the music teacher exam at the Academy. That's why he's rather late with his theology studies."

Henrik's face is closed, the blue eyes steadily on Anna's, expressionless. She turns her head away.

"I haven't really got anything else to say."

"And in what way had you thought things would be . . . in the future?"

"I don't know."

Tears come into her eyes, but force her anger away. Henrik smiles slightly.

"Why are you crying?"

"I'm not crying. But when you ask me what we are to do in the future, then I get angry. It's peculiar, but it is so."

"I'm trying to keep calm and . . ."

"Henrik! Our life together has gradually become alien and

36

incomprehensible. I have not been myself. I have been imprisoned."

"But together with Tomas, you're free. Is that so?"

"I haven't given a thought to whether I'm free or not."

"Anna?"

"Yes."

"What do you want more than anything else?"

"Are you asking me seriously?"

"Seriously, Anna."

His tone of voice is mild and he is looking at her without rancour or distance. She is confused and anxious. The emotions of the conversation are rushing in different directions and are ungovernable.

"You ask me what I want and I don't know. Perhaps I want to look after our home. I want to care for our children, of course. That's silly, I mean, anything else is inconceivable. I can stay with you, and I can help you with your work. I can be of great help to you."

"But Tomas?"

"There's no future with Tomas. He will gradually find his own way. He'll marry someone of his own age, someone who'll be a good wife and mother. But let me have a little freedom. Let me be together with Tomas. Only for a short time."

"A short time? What's that?"

"I don't know. You asked how I would prefer our life to be now and in future. And I am trying to answer."

"Do you mean that I should get hold of a 'lady' of some kind for this undefined future?"

"Please, Henrik, don't be ironic."

"I'm sorry."

. . . says nothing

. . . says nothing

. . .

"If you wish it, if you absolutely demand it, then I'm prepared to leave everything, our home, the children . . . everything."

" . . . and the children?"

"Yes, the children. One thing, Henrik, one thing is quite certain: you've always been good and loving with the children. You've been strict with the boys sometimes . . . much against my will. But perhaps things would be better for them if I'm not here. Then they would escape our difficulties . . . we've always kept the children out of them, haven't we?"

"Poor Anna."

"As you say."

"Poor Anna. Things are bad for you."

"Yes, they are. Sometimes I've prayed to God that I would fall ill, that I would end up in hospital, that I would be taken away from all this guilt, all this . . . guilt, yes. . ."

Henrik leans forward and takes her hand, holds it. He is grave, tender.

"Don't you think, Anna . . . mine, that there is some kind of meaning in what is afflicting us? And which hurts so terribly?"

Anna listens to his good voice, sees his face quite close to hers. He is no longer turned away. He is gentle, almost solemn.

"I've been on my way so many times. After all, you're my best friend, despite everything that's gone on. You're the only person I've ever been able to talk to, because it was so unreal going around apparently playing a part. Do you understand what I mean?"

"Yes, I understand."

"I was going to tell you everything, and together we would . . . But then I thought about what a dreadful lot you have to do, all that responsibility and all those people. Then I thought you wouldn't be able to take the truth, and it would be inconsiderate to drag you into something I had to sort out myself. Then the days just went by . . . and sometimes, quite suddenly, I thought: now! Now I'll say it. It doesn't matter what happens . . . but I could see how tired you were, how despondent, and then you talked about your fear of being inadequate, and I saw your terrible anxieties when you were to preach.

So nothing got said. And the more time that went by, the harder it became, of course."

"Does anyone know?"

"No."

"Not your mother?"

"How do you think I'd dare talk to Ma. No, no, impossible, Henrik."

"No one else, either?"

"No, Henrik."

"Are you sure?"

"I won't lie. It'll be difficult now. Märta knows."

"Oh, Märta."

"I'll tell you, so you know, but it'll hurt."

"Perhaps it's better if I know."

"This is what happened. I wanted Tomas and me to be able to be together. I wanted us to have a few days . . . and nights . . . together. He wanted to, and didn't want to . . . he was afraid and thought it would be deceit. I told him the deceit was already a fact. So I wrote to Märta. She was living temporarily in her aunt's house in Norway, near Molde. She answered at once and said we were welcome and she was going to a mission congress in Trondheim."

"Oh, I see."

"I see that you *want* to understand."

She lowers her head and kisses his hand. Then she sobs loudly, controls herself and runs her hand over her eyes and forehead.

"Have you confided in anyone else?"

"Yes."

"And . . ."

"Uncle Jacob."

"So now he knows."

"He's a friend of ours and is close to us. He confirmed me."

"He's my superior."

"Does that matter?"

"No, maybe not."

"He likes you, I know that. You know it, too. I met him suddenly and I was unprepared. We sat on a bench in the churchyard, talking together. He asked me straight out whether I had anything on my mind and I confessed."

She falls silent, frightened.

"And?"

"He advised me to tell the truth. He said there was no possible alternative. He said I should put an end to the relationship with Tomas. He said it was my duty, the only possibility. He said I was sinning against you if I didn't tell you. He was very stern."

The latter in a whisper, sorrowfully. Henrik leans back in his chair, letting go of Anna's hand and turning his head to gaze over at the dark rain-streaked window pane reflecting the oil lamp and two blurred hunched figures. The serious gentle calm is still there. Nothing strident, wounding. Open or tucked away. No.

"Oh, so you thought he was stern. What had you expected?"

"I don't know. I went into confession with no purpose or hopes. It was necessary. Perhaps I knew what he would say, but at the same time I was afraid."

"Were you afraid?"

"I said to Uncle Jacob that the truth in this case could be a disaster for a great many people. And he replied that it was wrong to underestimate you."

Silence. Then she goes on.

"And now I see that Uncle Jacob was right. And I'm grateful. You've helped me in a kind of life-and-death struggle."

She is weeping openly now and flings her arms round his shoulders, sliding down to her knees and pulling him to her and kissing his eyes and forehead and throat, and when he seeks her, she kisses his lips. He falls over her and for a brief moment she comes to her senses. Then she closes her eyes and is yielding.

A scarcely perceptible dawn. The rain has stopped but the clouds are moving heavily across the stillness of the bay. No wind until morning. Anna and Henrik are in his bed, and he has curled up with his cheek against her breast. He is sleeping uneasily, his breathing inaudible. She is wide awake, clearly awake with neither peace nor reprieve.

She cautiously frees herself from the uncomfortable deadlock and slips out of bed. She pulls the covers over his shoulder and for a long time looks down at the defenceless sleeping man.

She carefully eases open the sliding door to her own room, closing it soundlessly. She lights a candle on the bedside table and crawls down under the blankets. It is cold and damp, the window open and with no blind. The rain rustles and murmurs in the drainpipe and the rainwater tub. A bird lets out a quick cry far away, otherwise it is so quiet she can hear a faint buzzing in her ear. She closes her eyes and thinks she won't be able to go to sleep . . . perhaps, after all, she sleeps for a few moments, on this first morning of this new terrible life. Henrik has come into her room; clearly she has not heard him. He says her name very quietly, like a whisper. "Anna. I want to ask one last question which won't leave me in peace."

"Yes."

"Forgive me if I woke you."

"I don't think I was asleep."

"No, don't light the candle. I can see you. It's better like this."

"What did you want to ask?"

"Well, it's . . ."

He hesitates, has gone over to the window and is standing facing the floating soundless dawn.

"Say what you thought."

She is now sitting upright with clasped hands, observing the dark shadowy figure over there by the grey rectangle of the window.

"I want to ask you straight out. I've been about to many a

time. But haven't dared. Now I'm asking tonight from total honesty. And I beg you to be truthful."

"Yes, I promise."

"Was it a physical enjoyment to be with Tomas?"

"It was a physical enjoyment."

"Was it a greater enjoyment than with me?"

"You mustn't ask me that."

"I beg you to answer honestly."

"I can't."

"So, that's sufficient answer."

"I can't help that it is so."

"What is wrong between us?"

"I love Tomas."

"But you don't love me."

"Maybe, a long time ago. I don't know."

"But you've never had any enjoyment."

"I didn't want . . ."

"I want you to say it exactly as it is."

"No. I've never had any physical joy when you and I have been together. I've mostly wished to get it over and done with as soon as possible. Well, we've joked about that."

"We joked, yes, that's true."

"It was never a problem, anyhow, not for me."

"Only a little unpleasantness."

"More or less, yes."

"And not too often."

"Not too often, no, that's true."

"But with Tomas everything was different."

"You mustn't ask."

"Oh, I see. I understand."

"Please, Henrik, sit down here on the bed."

"No, no. I won't keep you awake any longer, Anna mine. You must be immensely tired."

"Yes."

"I'm tired, too."

42

"Goodnight, then, Henrik. Take my hand."

"Goodnight, Anna. No, no, no. It's all right like this."

He sounds distrait, sad. He opens the sliding door and carefully closes it again. Anna hears him moving about in the other room.

She stays sitting there, erect and unmoving, her hands clasped, her dry wide-open eyes on the dawn that never comes.

It is vitally necessary that I stop at this particular moment and think the situation over. Which way do the veins of the spring run? What does truth look like? . . . Not what it was like in reality. That's uninteresting. But just this: in what form does the truth appear, or . . . in what way are the main characters' thoughts, emotions, tendencies to anguish, and so on, repudiated and formed, or distorted for ever? I must stop and be wary: *You are inflicting a mortal blow. I am inflicting on you a mortal blow.* The spiritual landscape of the main characters is being exposed to a violent convulsion . . . like a natural disaster. On the whole, is it even possible to describe, and most important, is it not the long-term consequences to bodies, souls, minds and features which gradually become visible quite long after the actual collapse? Is a settlement of the kind now occurring particularly one of words? Won't it more likely be a fumbling, desperate and confused, both by the party pursuing (Henrik) and the one on the defensive (Anna)? Won't the scene reach the point where Anna's contrition turns to attack and righteous wrath? Perhaps not in what is called reality . . . in which this event extends over weeks, months and years, with grinding monotony, only occasionally broken by armistices and illusory reconciliations with pathetic assurances of ultimate peace. How to describe the *eternal circling*, the gnawing repetition, the repeated increasingly humiliating questions, which finally put an end to all compassion. How shall I describe the poisoning that imperceptibly fills the home like a nerve gas, corroding everyone's minds for lengthy periods, perhaps a lifetime? How do I portray the standpoints and partisanships that necessarily become blurred and uncertain when the participants on the second level never have the chance of a share in the factual truth? No one knows . . . everyone sees.

The next day is cloudy and windless, the rain has stopped but everything is damp. Not much is spoken between the spouses, both of them exhausted and unable to relax. Henrik goes out early in the old boat with a fishing rod. Anna writes some letters and sees to some accounts, then cycles to the farm where there is a telephone in order to phone her mother to hear how the children are. Karin has a sharp ear and notices that Anna's voice sounds different. She asks if anything has happened, which Anna unhesitatingly denies. The boy Dag has got a fish-hook stuck in his cheek and they have been to the cottage hospital in Repbäcken to have it taken out, other-wise nothing has happened, they are all well, the children rather down in the mouth because their summer visit and freedom have come to an end. They know the regime at Smådalarö is considerably stricter, but everyone is well.

Dinner for two is peaceful, with perch in white sauce and rhubarb crême. The quiet conversation is about urgent matters concerning the family (the hook in the cheek, of course, and what Ma thinks about the future for her daughter-in-law and her little son). Also about the parish work, the yet again postponed restoration of the church, Pastor Arborelius's com-plaints to the church council about the absence of the grant for the Baltic trip, the pleasing growth of the mothers' unions recently set up, and other such matters. After dinner, there is coffee on the veranda. A sudden ray of sunlight makes its way through the immobile mist below the clouds. The spouses point out together that the sun has come out so unexpectedly. Perhaps it'll be a fine day tomorrow, perhaps they can go out to

Skärholmsviken. Anna says this almost appealingly and Henrik smiles faintly and says that might be nice. Then all conversation runs out, all words evaporate, their voices, vocal cords, tongues, lips cannot cope. Silence. Anna is darning a sock, a large hole over the darning mushroom. A dying wasp buzzes behind the long rows of pelargoniums. The sun goes in after a few minutes, no wind, the light with no shadows, satiated with moisture. Henrik is reading the paper with greater care than usual.

At seven o'clock they listen to the news together. Then they move into the dining-room, light the lamp above the round table and Henrik reads a few chapters aloud from a new novel by Elin Wägner. They also take their habitual evening walk. At about ten, they wish each other goodnight, kiss cheeks and turn out the oil lamps. Henrik sits down on the veranda steps and smokes a cigarillo. The reflection on the water, the bay and the inlet can just be seen in the falling shadows ... first a long twilight, then a sudden autumnal darkness descending from the immobile clouds. Anna has retreated into her room and her thorough evening rituals, then the evening book, glasses on her nose, cuticles massaged and rubbed with healing ointment.

Nothing is said that day, the anaesthesia still complete. The next day comes with wind, wandering clouds and a taste of autumn and is just as calmly unremarkable as the previous day. In that way, Anna and Henrik are left to themselves and each other for three days.

The silence between the spouses has been acceptable. An outsider by chance observing their behaviour and tone of voice will hardly have registered anything deviant or alarming. Anna, usually the one to lance festering boils, does not dare move in any direction. Whatever she is thinking or feeling of anguish, rebellion, guilt, sorrow or anger she keeps to herself with a troublesome effort. At the same time she is uncertain and confused ... is this all? Will life simply slide back into habitual tracks? Or are these quiet days pregnant with an unfathomable threat?

Henrik moves and speaks cautiously so as not to be woken and made aware of an unendurable pain. Friendliness, brief breakthroughs of tenderness and tactful silences are the characteristics of those days.

Miss Lisen is to come on the midday boat at three o'clock on Friday. On Saturday at the same time, the children are to arrive, accompanied by the ever-helpful Miss Agda, who is really an elementary school teacher somewhere far out on the Upsala plain, but owing to her weak lungs, she nowadays enjoys a modest sickness pension and devotes her time to being the children's kindly and resigned governess.

When the spouses as usual have finished dinner at five o'clock, they help each other clear the table and do the dishes. In this connection, Henrik holds up a glass against the light from the kitchen window and points out that the glass is chipped. Anna is busy at the washing-up bowl and replies without emphasis that that certainly might well be so. Henrik does not at once reply but a few minutes later he remarks that the dinner service in general is in a deplorable state. Several glasses are chipped, some plates, too, and the cutlery does not match, some purely kitchen cutlery ... the words come one after another and are unclear. Anna is unprepared and answers patiently that when they had rented the house some of the household goods were included in the rent and she found it unnecessary to drag too much out from town. Henrik goes on drying cutlery and appears to be pondering on his wife's argument. At that moment, Anna is afflicted with the icy insight that their life is about to crack. Henrik says: "Yes, well, all that may be all right in itself. But I don't see why we have to sit at table with a dirty cloth. That I don't understand."

Dirty cloth? Anna stops washing up, takes her hand out of the bowl and with the back of it strokes a strand of hair off her forehead.

"The tablecloth is dirty. I don't know how many days the table has been laid with a dirty cloth . . . but it must be over a week, probably ten days. When I was on my own here, I didn't like to say anything to Miss Lisen. But it surprises me that you haven't noticed the stains on it. You usually observe such things."

Anna does not answer, but as she goes into the dining-room, she wipes her hands on her apron. She opens the sideboard cupboard, takes out the cloth and with a swift movement spreads it out over the table.

"Where are the stains?" Anna asks politely, but with an inner convulsion she finds difficult to control.

"There and there and there." Henrik points. Yes, there are three stains on the white cloth, but they are not entirely easy to find. A darker patch, a spot from candlegrease the size of a small coin, a rust mark out by the hem, and also a more noticeable mark, not particularly extensive, but visible.

"I can't understand what you're getting at," says Anna, summoning up all the calm she can muster. She sits down at the table and puts her hands palms down on the cloth. Henrik stays where he is, a flaring red patch on his right temple, his hand resting on the ornate back of the dining-room chair. His hand is trembling slightly.

"I don't understand what you're getting at, Henrik."

"Nothing special. Nothing important. Anyhow not to you, apparently."

"Tomorrow you will have your dinner served on a clean cloth, then the matter will be settled. I'm sorry if the chipped glass and the marks embarrassed you, but we are actually in the country and we have no guests."

"I don't regard the matter quite so simply."

"Then I think you should immediately say in what way you do regard the matter."

Anna manages a small smile. Henrik stays by the chair, tracing his forefinger along the woven pattern of the tablecloth.

"It's very simple, Anna. I suddenly realise that you've abandoned the home."

"What did you say . . .?"

"Abandoned our home. The fluff under the beds . . . the dead flowers, the torn curtain . . . there . . ."

Henrik points at the windows facing the veranda. One of the light white curtains shows a few threadbare places.

"But Henrik. I have been away for six weeks and Miss Lisen, however good she is, is beginning to see badly. We've discussed that. I can't help . . ."

"And why have you been away for six weeks?"

Anna is now helpless and looks appealingly at the man on the other side of the table. But he doesn't see her. He has lowered his eyes, or perhaps he has closed them. The red patch on his temple has spread. His hand is shaking almost imperceptibly.

"Answer honestly."

"I don't understand. We came to an agreement. You remember that Dr Fürstenberg ordered forest air for the children. You didn't want to go to Dalarna to stay with Ma. You wanted to be here by the sea. Don't you remember that *you yourself* suggested that the children and I should go to Dalarna and you would come here, then we would meet up again at the beginning of August. Have you forgotten?"

"What I happened to think of was how quickly you agreed to my suggestion."

"I was grateful for your generosity and that you raised no objections."

"You were grateful I gave you the opportunity to see your lover. I did wonder a little about the trips to Upsala, but now I know."

The tone of voice on both sides is courteous, Anna still appealing for reason and consideration, Henrik slowly and, for him, imperceptibly allowing himself to be carried beyond the limits of insight.

"I went with Ma to Upsala three times to help her clear up after Ernst."

"Four times, four, Anna."

"Oh yes, of course, that's true. Once we had to see to Carl. He had been making a nuisance of himself at his lodgings. We had to get him into Johannesberg Hospital at once. You know that."

"But they were all excellent excuses to meet your lover."

Silence.

"Answer me, Anna. For God's sake, let's be honest."

Silence.

"I urgently beg of you."

"What do you want? I've told you everything. What more do you want?"

"Details."

"Details. What do you mean?"

"Exactly what I say. You owe me a detailed account of your . . . your . . . love-making with that person."

"And if I refuse?"

"I have ample means of making you. Have you thought of that possibility?"

"Yes."

She *has* thought about it. She has also spoken about her apprehensions to Märta and Jacob. *He might take the children.* If it comes to separation or legal divorce, he would be given custody of the children. That is the law.

"So it would be better for us all if you try to be as honest as possible. I am asking you to answer my questions considerately and truthfully. Then in peace and quiet I shall put together your answers, possibly with a legally trained person, and consider what the next step should be. Do you understand what I am saying?"

"Yes."

"Did you wish to say something?"

"I was just wondering what had happened to all your

understanding and forgiveness. Where has your understanding from Sunday evening gone?"

"You cannot count on unalterable understanding. I was paralysed by what you had told me. Now that paralysis has begun to give way and I see where my duty lies."

"Duty?"

"Of course. My duty to the children. I must first and foremost think of the children."

"Henrik, Henrik, my dear."

"As you so clearly and inconsiderately have put your own pleasure first, thus jeopardising the existence of the family, then I must take the responsibility. It's quite simple. I cannot tolerate chipped glasses, dirty tablecloths and filthy curtains. I cannot tolerate the disintegration which you, through your . . . lewdness have allowed into our home."

"Henrik, you may not . . ."

"What may I not? I may. What I must do, what is my duty, at this moment, at this very moment. I must know everything, in detail. If you find it less distasteful . . . less embarrassing . . . I am prepared to formulate my questions in writing. Then you can answer me in the form of a letter, which naturally will be treated with the greatest of care. That is self-evident."

"No. Yes, I understand."

"I was here on my own, missing my family. I was pleased you were all having a good time. That the children were better. I wrote to say you should rest, that you should be happy and brave, that we would soon be seeing each other again, that we were in God's hands."

Anna is sitting with her face in her hands, not crying, but she has to conceal the anger moving heavily and exhaustingly in her vitals. I must be sensible now. I must think clearly. I must . . .

"What do you want to know?"

"Were you naked when you were together with that man?"
Silence.

"You heard my question."

"I heard your question, but may well wonder whether I am dreaming. This is utterly unreal, Henrik, my dear, my dear."

"It's a straight question. Were you naked? Were you naked?"

"Yes, we were naked."

"That's of interest, considering you only unwillingly show yourself naked when you are together with me."

"That's true."

"How many times have you been with that man?"

"I don't know."

"I'm sure you know. But you're ashamed to tell me how many times you've been together."

"Between fifteen and twenty times, I think."

"*How many times* have you gone directly from your love nest and immediately been together with me?"

"I don't know. I've tried to avoid it, but then I've thought that as long as it goes quickly, then it's better to give in than make a fuss."

"*That* is love!"

"Yes, perhaps that is love."

"And how long has this swinish behaviour been going on?"

"If by swinish behaviour you mean my loving relationship, then it has lasted just over a year. Last Midsummer, Gertrud and Tomas came to Våroms. You were to come a week or so later. Mamma had gone to stay with her stepsons and I was alone with the children. Then Gertrud and Tomas came and we celebrated Midsummer together. Then we took long walks in the forest. One day Gertrud had a sore throat and stayed at home. Tomas and I walked up to Djuptjärn. There's a deserted farm there. I asked him to come with me. I persuaded him."

"Are you with child?"

"No."

"Why is that?"

"After all that trouble with my insides after my last delivery,

I don't think I can get pregnant. Something has probably been damaged."

"In that case, why have you said I have to be careful? Why have you lied to me?"

"I have lied because the thought of your seed in my body was unendurable."

"But not him in your body?"

"No, not him."

"I see."

"What is it you see so suddenly?"

"I see why you have neglected your home over the last year. The chipped porcelain and dirty tablecloths, for instance."

"On the contrary. I've had such a guilty conscience, I've redoubled my efforts to do things well for you and the children. I've made special efforts in all directions in my work in the parish. I did everything I could, everything I could think of. You can accuse me of the very worst things, Henrik. But not of neglecting the home, nor my work in the parish, nor of my caring."

"And guilty conscience."

"Yes, that, too. But most because I loved you . . . yes, you, too . . . and wanted to keep you compensated. As much as I was able to."

"And what did you talk about?"

"Now I don't understand."

"What did you talk about, you and that man? For you can't have been whoring all the time."

"You may not use such words when talking to me."

Silence, then:

"I'm sorry, you're right."

"Not just anything, Henrik."

"But what did you talk about? He's taking exams to become a priest. He's a young man and is said to be an excellent musician. Pianist? or . . ."

"He wondered whether God would punish us."

"And?"

"I thought perhaps that I would be allowed to experience the joy of love for once in my life. Tomas was more worried than I was. I prayed to God that he would punish *me*, not Tomas."

"So you outbid each other?"

"What do you mean?"

"In religious eroticism. What a smacking of lips."

Anna stares at Henrik, speechless. The tunnel narrows, the safe foundations of reality collapsing into dust and ashes. There is no basis for anything any longer, no firm ground for feet. Anna gets up.

"I have to vomit."

She tries to walk calmly, but her stomach is violently bringing up bile and it fills her mouth. She clenches her teeth and reaches the slope behind the oak tree just in time, stands there with her hands against the thick trunk and is violently sick. Her body contracts, sweat breaking out at the nape of her neck and in her armpits, on her cheeks and forehead. I have never vomited like this before, she thinks indistinctly. The attack subsides, she wipes her lips but stays by the tree, the stench of vomit enveloping her.

She senses rather than sees Henrik in the twilight. He is holding a cup of water to her mouth. "Drink this. It'll help you. Do you want to throw up again, otherwise let's go indoors. You can lie on the sofa in the living-room. I'll sit with you. We won't talk. We must try to be calm. First and foremost, it's now a matter of thinking clearly. We must not make bad any worse. There you are, a cushion and blanket, that'll be good. I'll sit here and be quiet. I do believe it's beginning to rain again. I think I'll shut the veranda door. There we are, and then the lamp on the sideboard can be on so that we can see each other – if we want to, of course."

Third Conversation
March 1927

Anna's mother has come to Stockholm from Upsala for a few hours to meet her daughter. She has booked a room at Nylander's Guest House on the corner of Brahegatan and Humlegårdsgatan.

For a few weeks, Anna has been staying at a rest home with Henrik, who has been on leave of absence for six months (owing to "overwork and weak nerves" as it says in the medical report). It is inappropriate that Henrik and Anna's mother meet, hence this arrangement at the guest house.

It is an afternoon in March, 1927.

Anna in the street.

Anna in the entrance.

In the hall.

Miss Elin Nylander, with her white, well-brushed hair and her very dark eyes.

The long dark passage and then past the kitchen.

Miss Nylander apologises for not having a larger or better room, but all the rooms are taken until Easter. This concerns only for a few hours.

The room faces the courtyard and has a high narrow window, a pier-glass, a bed and two chairs, all white. And a wash-stand with a jug and bowl, the screen pushed to one side, a small writing table by the window. Karin Åkerblom is sitting there. She has taken a file out of the worn brief-case. Miss Nylander asks whether she requires anything. Karin has already had some tea. The tray is still on a chair and

Miss Nylander at once picks it up to take it out. No, Anna does not want any tea, so Miss Nylander closes the door and, of course, she never listens. She goes straight to the kitchen with the tray, turns off the gas under the kettle, then sits down to read the newspaper and lights a small Turkish cigarette to go with it.

In what way do Anna and her mother greet each other? Do they embrace, Anna quickly taking off her coat and hat and putting them on the chair by the door? Does she take off her overshoes, adjust her hair in front of the misty mirror of the pier-glass? What kind of gestures and tone of voice prevail during the first minutes of this shamefaced meeting between mother and daughter in a cramped room facing the courtyard in Miss Nylander's splendidly quiet guest house on this March day of falling snow and muddy streets? A child is crying down in the courtyard. Well, whatever it is like now, life goes on, it has to, it has to go on. So humiliating to have to meet in a cramped room in Miss Nylander's guest house.

"I haven't much time. Henrik's train from Upsala gets in at five o'clock. He was to take a taxi and by then I want to be at home. What had Professor Thorling got to say?"

"Not much. He listened carefully to my account and explained that he had read your letter carefully. But for natural reasons, he didn't want to say anything until he had spoken to Henrik."

"Couldn't he say *anything*?"

"Don't be so impatient, Anna. Professor Thorling is an experienced doctor. You can't expect him to accept our assertions once and for all. He was also very clear on one point. He can't have Henrik admitted to hospital against his will. The reasons for 'sectioning', as it's called, are extremely precise. The patient has to be a threat to himself or to other people."

"So something has to happen first before he can intervene?"

"The Professor was careful to point out that hitherto he has no evidence to show that Henrik could be mentally ill in the legal sense."

"But the damage done?"

"The damage?"

"To me, to the children. Doesn't the damage count?"

"Anna, come and sit down here opposite me, then we can try talk sensibly to each other. For the little while left at our disposal."

"I can't. I won't."

"Don't stand over there by the door. You look as if you're about to run away."

"How long am I supposed to endure this?"

"Sit down. That's better."

"Mamma! You know, everything goes round in circles. It starts with something we went over yesterday, and the day before and the day before that. How is it possible for a priest who has lost his faith to preach for Sunday after Sunday? *And* . . . it's my fault that he's lost his faith. How can I take it on my responsibility to drive him into a breakdown and destitution? *And* . . . if he doesn't sleep, it's because those evil thoughts have taken him over and convulse him so he starts weeping. Then I have to put on the light. And then? What is it going to be like for the *children*? A father, who can't get things right and is always ill? A priest who can't preach? And what will it be like when he's there in the pulpit and it's crowded with people and everyone's face is turned towards him? And then he has nothing to say? For he should tell the truth, and the truth is that I, Anna, his wife, or whatever they call me nowadays, that his wife has made him into such a wreck, he can no longer stand by what he preaches. That's what's happening, Mamma! And then there are the sleeping pills, and that he can't cope, hasn't the energy. Whatever I say, whatever I do, everything is poisoned. He looks at me with those vacant eyes filled with tears, tears of self-pity, and then he says he is *unworthy*. For he doesn't want to die. He is afraid of death, I've realised that and it is all meant to humiliate me. I am to be humiliated. And in the end, finally, I am the one to bear the blame, and at the same time, Mamma, at the same time he humiliates and violates me, I am to *console* him."

"I want to ask you something, Anna. And I want you to answer me honestly. When you married Henrik against my will and the family's, I foresaw difficulties, conflicts, tears. But now there's something that does not quite fit. But I was quite certain of one thing, and that was that he loved you. What has happened? What has changed his feelings? The reasons we can see are not sufficient basis for such a hideous about-turn."

"I don't understand what you're trying to say, Mamma."

"I'm sure you do. I want to ask you whether you consider you bear any of the blame for the present situation. Look at me, Anna! And answer me as honestly as you can. Are you in any way to blame for what is happening now, what is tearing you both apart and threatening the children?"

"Yes, some of the blame is mine."

"Then you must tell me."

"I won't submit to being robbed of my freedom. I won't submit to not being allowed to think as I want, feel as I want. A good friend of ours, a dear friend you know, Carl, Carl Alderin, is studying for his finals in law. Well, he tells me he won't be finished this spring and, of course, he's a careless creature. And then he says he won't be finished until Christmas. Then Henrik gets furious and writes to him and says that under such circumstances, he is not welcome in our home. And Carl telephones me and weeps and says he doesn't understand. And I have to refuse my home to that poor wretch."

Anna stops. She realises that this argument has not made the slightest impression on her mother. "Yes . . . well?" is all she says, looking at her daughter with her dark-blue eyes, her round face, high forehead, strong double chin, gleaming white hair so carefully put up. The whole little person sitting there opposite her daughter radiates energetic attention.

"Yes . . . well?"

"Don't you see, Mamma. Suddenly I am not allowed to receive a friend who is unhappy. Our mutual friend. He is to be punished."

"That's a reason to be annoyed, not for a tragedy. The reason, Anna?"

"I am imprisoned for life and I realise I'll never get away. But I refuse to be! I have no intention of giving way. I do not forgive. I am not understanding. I no longer love that man."

"Is there anyone else?"

"No . . . no."

The answer comes promptly. Anna meets her mother's eyes steadily and unhesitatingly. "How can you even think such a thing, Mamma?"

"You must forgive me for wondering."

Silence.

"Mamma, you were the one to bring me up to freedom. You were the one who demanded that I should have a proper professional training. You and Aunt Signe talked about a woman's right to a life of her own. How does this match up?"

"Three children change the conditions and put your own interest in second place. You know that."

"Yes."

"You must take the responsibility for the children's lives."

"That's exactly what I want to do. I want to break away, to take the children with me, to create a healthy and ordinary home. I want to go back to my profession. If I am destroyed, the children will be destroyed."

"You can't discount their father."

Silence again. Silence and silence.

"You say nothing."

"What can I say?"

"We were to speak honestly."

"When you produce those arguments, Mamma, I am struck dumb."

58

"Maybe there are reasons for that."

"There may be, but the reasons do not have to be the truth."

Silence, silence. Things are difficult now.

"Things are difficult now, Mamma."

"Yes, they are. Because you're lying. And I'm ashamed of your lying. I'm ashamed."

"What is there to know?"

"Quite recently, I was told that for three years you have had a relationship with a younger man. I know what his name is. I know who he is. I know his parents. But I shall not mention his name."

"How did you find out . . ?"

"That doesn't matter. Eighteen months ago, you told Henrik about it. The difficulties began with those circumstances. Almost exactly a year later, he has a breakdown and is taken to hospital. According to my information, owing to overwork. Is that right?"

"Yes."

"Do you still adhere to your relationship?"

"Yes, it's true."

"Henrik wishes to continue your marriage. He wants to take up his work again. He wants to try . . ."

"Yes, I know."

"You look on a continuation with repugnance and are planning a break?"

"Yes."

"The plan includes having Henrik certified as ill. You maintain he's mentally disturbed. You want him locked up so that you are guiltless to the world outside."

"Yes."

"You are initiating me into your plan. You tell untruths and you want me to help you."

"It was my only way out."

"I do not intend to comment on your behaviour. In the end, everyone has to stand by his or her own actions."

Anna laughs briefly and joylessly.

"That's what you usually say, Mamma."

That's it, distance, twilight, pale faces, breathing despite everything, pulses despite everything. Indistinct fury. You, who are my mother, you have never loved me. I went my own way, ways you, my mother, had indeed pointed out, but when I took you at your word and went those ways you pointed out but forgot, then you cut me out of your heart, then you didn't want to see me. I loved and admired you, but to no avail. That's what it was like then and so it is now.

And then, on the other side, there sits Anna, my daughter, my child, all the time giving me dark undisguised looks. I should reach out and touch her. That would be simple. Her wounds, after all, are my wounds. Why do I sit without moving and look at her with alien eyes, as if at a stranger? Why do I harden myself? Why do I erect obstacles? Why do I make irrelevant excuses for decisive points of principle? Why can't I . . . she has gone wrong. My dear child, why don't I take you in my arms, my little girl has always gone her own way. She has never listened but has cut herself off, turned away and shut me out, leaving me powerless and raging. Is this retribution? Is there any satisfaction in seeing her distress? No, no satisfaction. But no closeness, either.

Dusk, slow wet snow against the narrow window. Distant snatches of piano music, a few bars here and there. Anna looks at her mother, now turned to face the light descending from the well of the courtyard. Yes, unreal. Here in an alien room with an alien fireproof wall outside and alien emotions from nowhere. Habitual tones of voice, everyday touches and forms of address are far away, scarcely exist. What is happening? Where am I? And then love, exhausted and desecrated, now nothing but an ache. Weight, pain, ache. An illness with no cure. I just want to be . . . I thought I was unconquerable, that I was master over my reality. And then the weeping, but no tears.

"I'm going back to Upsala on the seven o'clock train. Go home to Henrik and the children. When do you have dinner? Oh, later today, when Henrik is back home, perhaps? Then we mustn't keep each other much longer. I would just like to talk to you about some practical matters, if you would give me a few more minutes."

Karin switches on the table lamp, puts her glasses on, opens the file and with a certain long-winded thoroughness, takes out a file of bills, some loose papers and a brown envelope.

"I've hunted everywhere for your address book, in the drawers in your desk, in your handbags and in the cupboard, but to no avail. Are you sure Henrik hasn't taken it?"

"I don't know."

"I've phoned Östermalm laundry as you asked, and reserved a time for you at the end of the month."

"Thank you."

"Then I must tell you that Ellen won't be staying. For that reason, I've cut short Evy's holiday. So she's already hard at it at home. But Ellen isn't staying. She's not only exhausted, but her trip back home has already been postponed twice. So she's extremely pleased to be back with me in the quiet of Upsala. It's better that Evy should start from scratch, now she's to take charge of the household. Maj has had a bad cold, but is up and about. You've a good girl in her and you can rely on her. But Ellen has gone. I presume you can't keep three helpers going?"

"No."

"Before coming here, I went to the Rörstrand shop and ordered six sideplates in the same pattern as those you have. They should be delivered next week."

"Thank you."

"The receipted bills are here in the file, the sums all entered into the household account book and added up. I made it agree to about three kronor."

"Thank you."

"In the envelope you'll find a few letters from Henrik to me which I think you should read. You asked how I came to know."

"Thank you."

"While I remember, I've left the big silver serving spoon to be mended and polished. Number one Humlegårdsgatan. It'll be ready in a month ... they've a lot of work on hand, but I thought if I didn't do it now, it would never get done. They promised the spoon would be as good as new."

There is nothing more to add. Anna gets up, goes over to the chair by the door, puts on her coat and stands there with her hat in her hand. She wants to say something but words fail her.

"Anna!"

"Yes."

"Come over here."

Anna obediently goes over to her mother, stands in front of her like a child, her head lowered, her eyes inaccessible.

"What do you want to say?"

"I don't want us to part on bad terms."

"Nor do I. On the contrary, I'm tremendously grateful for everything you've done for me over this long and difficult time. I can't even imagine what would have happened if you hadn't been able to help. So I'm profoundly grateful. It was stupid of me not to tell you about my relationship with Tomas. That was stupid of me. Especially as I ought to have reckoned on Henrik telling you. That's obvious. By telling you, Mamma, he could hurt us both. That must have been satisfactory from many points of view. Dear Lord, dear Lord, how I hate him. I wish he was dead."

Anna is speaking calmly, largely as affirmation. "He follows me like an injured animal. He says he will never leave me. He says he will never leave me. He says he will put up with me living with Tomas. At the same time, he looks in my hiding places, reads my letters, listens when I'm on the telephone. And then he looks at me with those watery eyes which I hate so, and then he speaks to me in that quiet voice. Do you know, Mamma, he rummages in my books and extracts deletions and notes. He's even gone through my prayer book. Sometimes he seems to have come from Hades. But that isn't the worst. No, the worst is our sleepless nights. He comes into my bedroom at about one o'clock in the morning and wakes me up. Then he's taken sleeping pills, strong ones. And he lies on the floor and twists and turns and whimpers, or sits, just sits on a chair inside the door with his mouth open as if wanting to scream or vomit. It's so awful, I feel like laughing. Supposing he's *acting tragic?* Supposing he just wants to frighten me into contrition and compassion? And I say I'll do anything to calm him down. And then comes *that* ritual. If this is to be my life in future, then I'll refuse and leave, turn on the gas or cut my wrists . . ."

The cramped high room is lit by the yellow shaded lamp on the bedside table by the white bed with its crocheted bedspread and high ends. Otherwise it is fairly dark now, the March dusk outside like iron. It has stopped snowing, the fireproof wall looming against the dirty reflection from town. Down in the courtyard, two women in large coats, jugs in their hands, their overshoes deep down in the slush, are talking. Lights go on here and there in kitchen windows. Karin stays seated on the chair, her left elbow resting on the glass top of the dressing-table, her face turned to the window, expressionless.

Anna stands where she's been placed, opposite her mother, her hat now on the chair. She stands there in her suitable fur-trimmed coat, her hands in her pockets, her dark eyes wide but her voice calm, controlled as if she were talking about some third person with whom she was only slightly acquainted.

Karin has let her daughter go on, though it is uncertain whether she is listening to the words being spoken or whether she is just catching the tone of voice. I don't really know. No, she neither interrupts, nor looks at Anna, but lets her go on.

"In September when he had a breakdown that Sunday after

his sermon, he didn't want to see me. He refused to talk to me and turned away. I was given messages. Mostly from Miss Terserus. You know her, Mamma. She immediately took Henrik's side. It was she who saw to it that he was admitted to the Samaritan Hospital. It was she who spoke to Professor Friberger. It was she who arranged his leave of absence. It was she who told me that Henrik couldn't cope with speaking to me, that he hadn't the energy to see me. I was frightened to death at first. I was afraid he would do something. I don't know what I thought. And everything was my fault. I was sick with guilt. Then I was furious and threw all that overboard. I thought it was good not to have to see that man who had tormented me for a whole year, since last summer when I told him. Then all went quiet. I knew he was well looked after at the hospital. He had doctors and friends. I had reports through Torsten Bohlin and Einar. Then a period of time went by. I started to establish myself with the children and things were all right for us, calm and good. The boys were calmer, too, no sleepless nights and no nail biting, no noisy squabbles or fighting.

"Then the letters started, at first one or two a week, and then gradually every day, mostly accounts of daily events, how he was, who had been to see him, and what the professor had said. Then gradually the letters became more and more personal. Henrik started talking about wanting to move from Stockholm. He wanted to apply for a country parish somewhere far up in the north. He started talking about *our future.* His tone was forgiving, a troubled tenderness. He wrote that he missed me and the children. I asked Professor Friberger how I should behave and he urgently advised me to be as accommodating as I possibly could. Oh yes, I began answering his letters. At first fairly simply, then more exhaustively, then gradually with a kind of considerate dishonesty. I made myself do it, the only possible thing to do. And that went quite well. He came home for Christmas, you know that, and that went quite well, too. He had tranquillisers all the time and was tired but friendly. We celebrated Christmas almost as usual. It was a kind of ghostly play, but it worked. The day before his return to hospital, there was an almost irretrievable disaster. We all had Sunday dinner early. Henrik was to go back to hospital on the half past six train. Everything was packed and ready. Dag was sitting on Henrik's right, making rather annoying faces. He picked up his glass of water and drank it in the way Pastor Konradsen drinks his schnapps. He usually does that rather well and earns himself a well-deserved laugh. This time it all went wrong. The water went down the wrong way and he coughed and spluttered, dropped the glass and it broke, bits of glass and water scattering all over the table. Henrik reacts very violently to sudden noises and said sharply to the boy that he must watch his behaviour. Dag didn't answer, but picked up a spoon and banged it down on his plate. Henrik was furious and ordered him to leave the table. Dag sat in silence for a moment, then said calmly: 'That's good, then I don't have to see you, Father. We all think that, for that matter.' '*What* do you all think?' Henrik says, also calmly. 'All of us here think it's a good thing you're going back to hospital.' Then he got up and left the table, but slammed the door hard behind him. There was a terrible scene. Henrik went after Dag. We heard horrible screams from the children's room. He thrashed the boy with a carpet-beater. We stayed at the table as if paralysed. Gradually the screams subsided and I went to the children's room. Dag was lying face down on the floor, quite silent now. Henrik had gone into his study and locked the door. The boy was . . . bleeding, battered, skin peeling off him. I can't talk about it . . .

"Then Henrik went back to hospital. We did not speak. No letters came for a long time.

"Uncle Jacob received Henrik's formal resignation. He no longer wanted to be a parish priest as he considered himself useless and burnt out. Uncle Jacob went to see him in hospital and asked him to put off his resignation. After much talk hither and thither and a great deal of anguish, he promised not to carry out his decision. He talked about how we had matured through suffering and emerged cleansed from our trials. I didn't know what to say and went on telling half-lies. I silenced my fears for the future. I silenced my anxiety, well, I took what joys were available. And I met Tomas as often as I could. That wasn't all that often, but it didn't matter. It was anyhow all totally unreal. Or the moments with Tomas were also the only reality and everything else was unreal. I'm not all that sure. At the beginning of March ... well, you know now, Mamma ... Henrik and I went to Solgården. He was considered 'fit'. Well, you know that, Mamma. The sleeping tablets and the tranquillisers were to be reduced and he was slowly to get used to an ordinary everyday life together with me ... well, you know, Mamma. Professor Friberger went to America to lecture at some university and so Professor Thorling was to take over, and I suppose that wasn't exactly a catastrophe but ... well, you know that. You've talked to him. But you don't know what it was like up there in Solberga. I couldn't write and tell you because Henrik supervised my correspondence and demanded to read my letters. It was like being in hell. Outwardly, to other guests, to the matron and staff, he was charming, obliging, apparently happy and harmonious. It was horrible to see. In the long run it becomes confusing, Mamma, I promise you, because you think he is *capable* of appearing to be quite well, friendly, kind, amiable and happy. He is *capable* of it, after all. Well, I don't know, but I think about my own duplicity and the necessity and what would happen if I allowed myself to crack up? If I ... if I started to scream? Why should Henrik ... *Is* he a sick man – is he so hopelessly ill, he'll never get better? Does he *really* know he's ill? Or is it a game to gain advantages and power over other people, over me? No, I don't think it's conscious. I don't believe that. He's not that infamous. I don't want to believe that. And then you had good reports from Solberga all the time. Except that one letter I managed to smuggle out because he had gone on and on at them to give him a sleeping tablet. That letter. I can see it was confusing. I don't think we'll get any help from Professor Thorling. Henrik will charm him and seem happy and full of energy and the desire to go back to work. That's what it's like. There's no way out, Mamma. I sometimes wonder how much terror and tension and hopelessness a human being can take before breaking. Oh yes, I manage and keep on managing. And the days go by. But what for? What is the innermost point? Is there some hidden pattern that I'm not allowed to see through? Am I to be punished? Am I to be granted forgiveness, or is the punishment for life? And why do the children have to be punished for my crime? Or is it that my punishment is the children's suffering? I am far far away in the darkness, Mamma. And there is no sign of light. If there is a God, then I must be an eternity away from that god. So . . ." (falls silent)

"You were going to say something."

"So I go on seeing Tomas. I can see he's afraid. He has fallen in love with a maternal and agreeable older woman, who listened to his thoughts and his music. He was so trusting and loyal. And then quite suddenly . . . well, it's almost comical . . . ageing, lecherous, terrifying . . . clutching at him. Perhaps he wants to be rid of me although he doesn't dare . . . dare see . . . doesn't dare send me away, although I beg him to . . . *Tomas, dear, put an end to it!* Go, leave me, if I am doing you harm. I don't want to ruin your life. I am saying all this, but it's nothing but words. I'm not honest with him, either. For I really want to cry out to him all those crazy banalities . . . don't go, don't leave me, I'll leave everything, whatever you like. I'll leave the children and my life, as long as you take me to you and I may be with you. *That's* the truth. It's not exactly the whole truth, because I'm so ridiculously critical. They say love is blind, but it's not blind at all . . . love is sharp-eyed and hears everything. And sees and hears more than you want to hear or see. And I see that Tomas is a nice boy, with warmth and emotions and joy. But he's rather sentimental and often says silly things I pretend not to hear. And then I think about what it would be like if he and I . . . it wouldn't work at all . . . for he's just a little, just a little false and I can hear when he's lying. But I don't want to embarrass him, so the game starts. I sometimes wonder . . . I wonder whether I am truthful at that very moment. And then the actual truth fades away and disappears and can't be found. Mamma, I'm so confused. I talk and talk mostly because I'm just frightened and tired."

There's a knock at the door. Without waiting for an answer, Miss Nylander sticks her pale white-powdered face round and says: "It's the telephone. Out here in the hall. This way."

"I gave the telephone number to Evy should anything crop up," says Karin, but Anna doesn't hear that. She is already on the phone. "Hullo, it's me. Yes, of course, thank you, I'm glad you rang, Evy. I'll come at once. I'll be home in ten minutes. Yes, thank you, it's all right."

When Anna comes back into the room, Miss Nylander is there talking to her mother. She swiftly retreats and closes the door behind her, her dark eyes glinting faintly with well-brought-up eagerness. "Shall I perhaps ring for a cab?" she says outside the door.

"No, thank you, that's not necessary."

Then Anna turns to her mother and says that Henrik has come home earlier than expected and what shall . . .

"But my dear child, you've only been in town and come home and are surprised, that's . . ."

"Mamma, you must come with me. Otherwise Henrik'll believe, well . . ."

"No, I've no intention of meeting Henrik. I wouldn't dream of it."

"What shall I do? What shall I do?"

"Go at once, Anna."

She stands there looking in despair at her mother, who is

68

holding quite hard on to her arm. Then she lowers her head, takes her hat off the chair and turns to the mirror.

"Have a care, my dear."

That comes suddenly, perhaps equally surprisingly to both women. Anna flings her arms round her mother, who doesn't return the embrace, but pats her daughter on the back.

They stand like that for a few moments. Then Anna quickly leaves, nearly forgetting her handbag. Her mother points at it and Anna nods dumbly.

So. Now Karin is alone in the little guest-house room. The piano music far away inside behind walls and floors plays the last bars of a Beethoven sonata with wild precision. She covers her eyes with her hand. It is not true she is crying. All things of that kind have been put away, but it is probably grief.

FROM ANNA'S DIARY

Help me away from myself. Free me from this self who wants to think, wants to live, wants to love according to my own will. Obliterate, burn, annihilate this self of mine, for otherwise my lot will be only to destroy other lives and make others unhappy.

Fourth Conversation
May 1925

Anna is reading aloud.

"Molde is exceedingly beautifully situated with a magnificent view over the fiord and the snow-covered Romsdal mountain. The houses are for the most part wooden and deeply embedded in almost southern lush vegetation. During the summer, Molde is the centre of singularly lively tourism. The community was granted its charter as a town in 1742 and was severely ravaged by fire in 1916."

They have already travelled far, each going their separate ways. The agreed meeting place is Åndalsnäs, where the railway line from Oslo ends. Tomas has been waiting a day or two, staying in a guest-house down by the harbour. So they are going to undertake the last part of the journey to Molde together on board the little coastal steamer called the *Otterøy*. Tomas meets the night train, which arrives on time. They have time for a quick breakfast at the guest-house, but are both so on edge over their risky enterprise, they are scarcely able to eat a thing. After that they are able to walk at a leisurely pace to the quay. Anna's suitcase is in the charge of a porter. Tomas has already taken his insignificant luggage on board.

A brisk wind is blowing off the sea, the ship's bell rings, the gangway is drawn in, the mooring ropes cast off. The little steamer cautiously eases away from the quay between fishing boats, merchant ships and sailing boats. Inside the dim, plush-covered saloon smelling of mould, Anna has found a booklet about their journey's destination, Molde, at the far end of the fiord.

The journey has long been discussed, for several months, but has now actually come about. Officially, Anna is on a visit to her friend Märta Gärdsjö, who has long since been her only confidant.

In Molde, missionaries from all over Scandinavia have assembled for a congress, a hundred or so men and women from missions in Africa and China. Märta has just come back from the Congo and is temporarily living in her aunt's house. Quite some time ago, she has suggested that Anna should come and stay with her for a few days. When Anna cautiously asked in a letter whether Märta had any objections to the possibility of Tomas being in the town at the same time, Miss Gärdsjö wrote to say that he was welcome, and also that the congress had been moved to Trondheim, where an ecumenical service was to be held in the Cathedral. In its turn, this entailed Anna and Tomas having two days to themselves in the old house. Märta's aunt, the widow of a town councillor, was staying at a watering place in the Tyrol for her rheumatism.

There are not many passengers on board. At this particular moment, they are alone in the little saloon. Anna has put the guide book aside. Her hand seeks his. She closes her eyes, possibly wondering what she is feeling and establishing with some surprise that she feels nothing whatsoever. Possibly a hollow feeling of hunger, as she has not been able to eat any breakfast.

Then they are out on the fiord and the sea glints in the showers and the headwind, the ship dips and the windows are rinsed with spattering silvery water. The shiny brass lamp swings leisurely in its hanging bracket, the ship creaks, and women's voices can be heard through the wall to the refreshment room where they are laying the tables for dinner.

Tomas has a boyish face, open, candid with friendly eyes, brownish-blue. His mouth is large and obstinate, his nose strong, ears small and girlish. His hair is thick and brushed straight back off his high forehead. He is tall and gangling, with the large hands of a pianist. He bites his nails. His neat suit is rather worn and appears outgrown, reinforcing the impression of boyishness. He smiles easily. His voice is that of the well-controlled and expressive instrument of a musician. He speaks quickly and is very articulate.

Anna is wearing a skirt and blouse with a wide turned-down collar and a gold medallion on a thin chain round her neck. The sleeves are wide, the cuffs the same colour as the blouse. The skirt is ankle-length and her belt broad with an embroidered pattern and leather clasp. Her hair is as usual at this time with a centre parting, but newly washed, therefore unruly. Her cheeks are red, as if she were feverish. She feels her cheek with the back of her hand. It is hot. She is sure to have a temperature.

Right up to the last, Tomas had wished she wouldn't come, that she would be ill, that one of the children would fall sick, that Henrik's journey would be cancelled. At the station, he was walking back and forth an hour before the night train from Oslo was due in. Sincerity was hardly the most marked feature of his character. But now he was at once to turn to her and say, well ... say what? Then the train came thundering in and the ground shook just like himself. Then the long snake of carriages stopped in the clear wet light, steam puffing heavily out of the engine and between the carriages, and people moving busily and purposefully to and fro through the steam along the stone-laid platform. Tomas considered fleeing. This was his last chance of avoiding something overwhelming that would perhaps destroy him. But. She appeared behind his back. She called to him cautiously, as if sensing his terror and not wanting to frighten him any more. When he turned round and found her right close to him, his terror ran out of him. She was quietly serious and stood there quite calmly, or so it seemed, and then she smiled a little and indicated her bags to the right and left of her neat little person. "We'd better get a porter, yes, exactly. There's one. Good morning, these two cases are to go to the Molde boat which leaves at two o'clock. Shall I pay you now? No? Then we'll meet at the boat?" The porter heaved the cases up on to the small cart with other cases on it and wrote "Molde" on them with chalk.

That settled, they again face each other, smiling and serious. Well, then, perhaps we should greet each other? Hullo, Tomas dear. Hullo, Anna. They hold out their hands.

"It was kind of you to come and meet me. We said we'd meet on the boat."

"I've been waiting for several hours. Two, I think."

"So I suppose you were hoping I wouldn't be coming?"

Anna laughs suddenly and hurriedly strokes his cheek with her gloved hand. "Ah well, let's go then," she says firmly. So they go.

The engine thumps. Slowly, dipping, the creaking wood-work of the saloon. The voices in the neighbouring room. The water spattering against the windows.

"Do you get sea-sick?" says Tomas.

"No, I don't think so. Once long ago, I crossed the English Channel with Mamma and Ernst in a hurricane. Everyone was sick except Ernst and me."

"Your mother, too?"

"Yes, she was, just imagine."

Silence. Intimacy.

"Tomas, I think we must discuss a few *practical details*."

"I imagine that might be necessary."

"As I wrote to you, we are invited to stay at Märta's aunt's house outside town. Märta has been a friend of mine since we were girls at training school in Upsala. She is the only one who knows. She'll be away for the next few days and has left the key with an old woman who lives down by the harbour."

"Isn't that a good thing?"

"No, I don't think so. I don't want to involve Märta in our drama, should anything happen. I want us to stay in a hotel. That's sufficiently impersonal surroundings. What do you say?"

"I don't know, this suddenly."

"So I've booked rooms at the Town Hotel – one double and one single."

"But I probably can't . . ."

"Tomas! This is my affair. You insisted on paying for your fare. That's quite enough."

"Aren't you afraid?"

"If I think about it, I'm afraid. So I don't think about it. I don't plan to think. The only thing that frightens me . . ."

"Well, tell me."

"The only thing that frightens me at the moment is that we have to give overwhelming proportions to our love to justify what we're doing. Our love maybe can't cope with such a burden?"

"Is that what you think?"

She grasps his hand, brings it up to her lips and kisses it.

"You've a good hand, Tomas. At first, I mean before, I looked at your hand without you knowing and then I thought *that hand* . . ."

"Yes."

"I won't say it. Now let's talk about another practical matter."

She lets go his hand and reaches for the bag beside her on the bench, opens it, searches and finds a small wallet, opens a closed compartment and holds up a wedding ring between her thumb and forefinger.

"This is my maternal grandfather's wedding ring. He gave it to me as a souvenir. You can borrow it for a few days. It would be wrong if Pastor Egerman did not wear a wedding ring. It might be noticed by the hotel staff."

"You think of everything."

"You sound sad."

"No, no. But the ring . . . I don't know."

"Be sensible now, Tomas. The ring is a practical affair, nothing more. Rather fun, too. I wonder what Grandfather is saying in his heaven."

"That his grandchild is a godless, ferocious and dissolute heathen."

"Take the ring now, Tomas."

"Is there anything else?"

"I've a letter to Märta here. In it I thank her for her thoughtfulness, but that we don't need her house."

The ring is left lying in her open hand. He hesitates. Firmly, she puts the ring on his finger . . . a slight impatience.

"Now we'll draw the cloak of invisibility around our two days. No one knows. No one sees. Like in a dream. We'll have to see to it ourselves that it doesn't become a nightmare."

"Are you crying?" says Tomas, almost inaudibly.

"I hardly ever cry. I stopped doing that a long time ago."

"I've also longed for you."

"Sometimes I think: poor Tomas mine, he's probably appalled at all these emotions. His emotions and Anna's. If he's been longing, then maybe it was for something else . . . I don't know, perhaps something quiet, beautiful, free of lies. Not like this, no, I *won't* cry. I'm not sad, really. There's no need to console me."

He puts his arm round her shoulders and pulls her to him. She lets it happen, but almost at once frees herself. "No," she says decidedly, shaking her head. "No. I really must not complain. Now I'm living the best hours of my life. Come on, let's go out and look at the waves and the storm and the mountains. There's sure to be a wind shelter in the stern. Come on, Tomas."

The steamer *Otterøy* puts into two harbours before her ultimate destination, which is Molde. At first she turns west and goes into the deep narrow Langfjord. Furthest in is a small community called Eidsvåg, where they stop for an hour for loading and passengers, after which they go out through the fiord, turn north and head for the fishing village of Vetyy. Finally the little boat sets course for Molde and is calculated to reach port that evening.

75

Tomas and Anna have been alone in the little saloon. They have dozed a little, woken, dozed again, curled up in the soft red mould-smelling plush, wrapped in their coats.

Then the steamer is at the quay in Eidsvåg and it's raining quietly. The mountain shelters it from the wind. The noise of the few passengers and the crew, the tramp of feet and shouted orders reach them indistinctly through the stillness.

Then, however, there are footsteps outside the saloon. Someone knocks determinedly on the door and the intruder does not wait for an answer but comes in and stands inside the door.

It is a tall woman of about forty, dressed in the stern uniform of a deaconess. Umbrella, high overshoes. Gloves. Voluminous handbag. Her face is large and open, the forehead high, her hair drawn straight back, her eyes wide open and very blue. Strong well-proportioned nose. Her mouth is inconsistent, in the middle her lips soft and shapely, but that stops at the corners, where everything becomes determination. The lady is not beautiful, but attractive. When she smiles (and she is doing that at this very moment) she becomes almost amiable. Anna's forehead turns scarlet. Tomas expresses nothing, possibly mental short-circuiting.

"Märta!" says Anna.

"The very same," replies Märta, leaning her umbrella against a chair, her bag on another, her gloves on the bag, then taking off her uniform hat, putting it on the table beneath the lamp and finally unbuttoning her long coat. While she is carrying out all this, she is talking in her broad Småland accent: "Hullo, Anna, hullo, Mr Egerman. I imagine you're surprised, but nonetheless you look well and happy. And your cheeks are red, too."

She embraces Anna swiftly and awkwardly, and shakes hands with Tomas, who has risen to his feet and knocked over a tea cup.

When all that has been settled, they stand there for a moment, not reflectively, but simply in confusion. "Shall we sit down?" Anna suggests uncertainly. "Would you like some tea? I'll order some. They have bread and butter and things to go on it, as you see. You can have my cup for that matter, if you'd . . ."

"No, thank you. I came a few hours ago and took the opportunity to have a good tuck-in at a guest-house, no thanks. On the other hand, if you don't mind, Mr Egerman, I would like to talk to Anna alone. Have you got a cabin? No. I thought as much. So I've actually bought a cabin ticket, then Anna and I can withdraw for a while. Perhaps you could stay here in the saloon, Mr Egerman, and read a book. You can borrow the book I've brought with me to read on the journey."

She takes a thick tome out of her large bag. "Here you are. I'm sure you haven't read it, Mr Egerman. It's Søren Kierkegaard's *Acts of Love*, from 1847, translated, recently published with a commentary by Torsten Bohlin."

"If we have anything to discuss, I'd like Tomas to be present. That's necessary."

"The only absolutely necessary thing is that you and I can talk alone."

Anna looks at Tomas with astonishment, but lowers her head as a sign of agreement. The two women leave the saloon after Märta has rather laboriously gathered up her belongings. When the door closes and the two figures have disappeared from sight, Tomas is irresolute for a few moments, then throws himself down on the bench, puts his hands in his trouser pockets and quietly whistles a largo. Then he closes his eyes and listens to the pulse beating behind his ear and the engine vibrating far down below in the bowels of the ship.

They have left the harbour and are getting up speed. The strong May light breaks out, the raindrops on the saloon windows sparkling. Sudden trembling, sudden sorrow: "This is not me. This does not belong to me. I am poor, remain poor, poorer, poverty-stricken. Blessed are the poor in spirit? Are we really so blessed?"

*   *   *

"I took the fast boat at six this morning to intercept you two. I wanted to hand you the key personally so that Mrs Beck wouldn't be involved and start asking questions."

"We've just decided to book into a hotel. I've already booked rooms. I don't want to stay with Tomas in a strange house with strange rooms and strange furniture. You must understand! This is the first time and perhaps the only opportunity we will be allowed to be alone together."

"How can you possibly think that a hotel room in the town's main street with its thin walls, inquisitive staff and scoffing penetrating looks, how can you think that that would be better than the quiet of that old house in its big garden?"

Anna is sitting on a low stool, her back pressed against the wall, her head down. She is playing with an ornamental button which has come loose from a cuff.

The cabin lurches softly, the window occasionally drenched by the bright green water.

"I think I'm prepared," says Anna.

"Prepared, what do you mean, prepared?"

"Ten years ago. It was a cloudy day at the beginning of September. I was standing in the parsonage window facing the river, the river as black as ink. The snow started falling straight down. It was quiet all round me, everywhere, not a soul. I was alone in the world. Henrik and I were being terrible. He said nothing day after day. I veered away and turned my back. We had been married for two years. Two years, Märta, and we had a little boy. I was standing in the window in the silence, and I realised, you see: *realised* the whole depths of what I had done. I remember very clearly thinking that this is not my life and that man is not my husband and the only creature who has any rights to make demands on me is that little boy asleep in his basket in the bedroom. I saw that everything had to be unravelled. It was utterly clear . . . I felt a kind of joy. I felt I could

78

cope. I could really cope with everything I wanted to. There would be tears and torments. But I wouldn't submit. I no longer intended to stand glaring at that fretful averted man. I no longer intended to allow myself to be humiliated by those whining, petty-minded remarks. I was twenty-six and knew in one decisive moment what I wanted my life to be like.

"So I took the little boy with me and went to Upsala. Naturally, I imagined Ma would be pleased. For years she had been negative towards Henrik and our marriage. I thought I had come home. But I was mistaken. Mamma said almost at once that of course I could stay for a few days, but she had no intention of housing a runaway wife and that my obvious duty was to go back to Henrik and that I had made my choice and that one chooses *once* and there was no other choice. After three days, I went back. Two years later, in the spring of 1917, I made another attempt to escape. That time Henrik came and fetched me back and then we moved to Stockholm. I won't exaggerate. And I don't want to be unjust. Our everyday life has not been hell. We became like two cart-horses together pulling a heavy load. My lack of freedom has not been all that insufferable. That's not what I mean. But then Tomas appeared. That was just about a year ago, yes, Midsummer last year. And then followed what they call adultery. Suddenly there was no time to stop and draw breath. Then this trip. You mustn't think it's a hastily thought-up whim. This trip . . . well, I don't know how to express it . . . this is to do with death. Oh, now I've no words for what I want to say. But isn't it true that it's painful to discover one's loneliness . . . I mean *utter loneliness*, the loneliness at the moment of death, the loneliness of the child. I know, Märta! You're never alone. You live in the hand of God. No, *alone* . . . that's actually clear. And then Tomas came into my loneliness. And now both he and I can say: we are not alone."

She laughs. "What can I say? Is it worth saying anything except that I'm in a good mood. I'm *not* well. I'm sleepy, at the

79

moment I'm happy, give me your ball, then you can borrow my doll. I'm sad, but it's probably not worth saying 'I'm sad', because no one cares."

"When I left Molde this morning," says Märta. "I had my bags full of opinions, I don't think moralistic opinions, no, strangely enough I haven't had them all the time. No, I was curious to know what Tomas looked like . . . I remember him as a small boy, you see. His mother was also to be a deaconess and we were contemporaries. Then she married and then Tomas arrived . . . well, that's nothing to do with it. I was curious about what your Tomas had become as an adult. And then I wanted to give you the key. I just hoped you would get home unscathed, and you and I would make a plan in case anyone thought of asking questions. Then I also really wanted to see you. I think of you as my little sister whom I have to look after. I'm also a little jealous, I suppose. Well, I mean I'm a little jealous of Tomas. But you needn't take any notice of that. So it was probably stupid of me to come haring over like this. But rather typical, I think. I'm so incredibly understanding and then I thunder away. You must forgive me."

"Please, Märta, give me the key."

"What? The key?"

"No, don't ask me. Please give me the damned key."

"I've got in everything you might need, as it's Saturday. There's wood for the tiled stoves and coal for the kitchen stove and paraffin for the oil lamps."

Anna takes the key and puts it into her bag.

"Then let's go back to Tomas. He'll be wondering."

"I'll be back from Trondheim on Tuesday morning. Then I'll take over the house."

Anna embraces her friend. They stand close to each other and rock together tenderly and consolingly.

The Borkman house lies a few kilometres outside town at the foot of the mountain. The building is a result of the 1800s' faith in the future and architectural delight. The extensive but uncared for park is populated with dubious copies of classical statues. Some ancient fruit trees are already in bloom, the sanded paths covered with last year's leaves, and spring flowers glow in the flower beds along the south wall of the house.

They go round the house and Anna unlocks the kitchen door. It is seven or thereabouts on the Saturday evening. The rain has stopped, the wind has dropped and a harsh chill is pouring down the steep mountainside. In the distance the deep roar from the waterfall is audible, out of sight but nevertheless present. The sun sinks below the mountain, but is still shining strongly on the cloud formations in the west, the May light soft with no shadows. All this together with the worn elegance, scents of old sorrows and long since dead bouquets of roses in great over-furnished rooms gives Anna a sudden feeling of ruin. There is electricity . . . sleepy carbon-filament lamps giving out pale yellowish light and mercilessly revealing the shabbiness of the house . . . a hopelessly passé grandeur.

They sink down into a far too soft sofa in the drawing-room with its high heavily draped windows facing the dusk of the garden and the blossoming fruit trees. They hold hands. Well, now we're far away. So we've realised our dream. Or is this the demons' ingenious version of our dream? Are we actually present or has our boldness made us breathless and our faces pale? What is happening to us? Have we walked into a trap, approved with kindness and prudence by a dear friend? Is this ridiculous? Shall we laugh or is it already time to cry?

In this rising distress, which is not at all elegiac, Anna becomes practical. "I think we need something to eat and most of all something to drink. I remember Märta saying something about two bottles of wine she had put in the refrigerator. Come on, my dear, let's offer some resistance. We are not to be executed at dawn, are we? We're actually on a *pleasure* trip, Tomas."

Anna laughs at the sight of their miserable expressions she can just make out in the gilt-framed, fly-spotted drawing-room mirror. Anna laughs and Tomas also has to laugh despite his terror. They stand hand in hand and regard the testimony of the mirror. With what they see and the sudden joy, their closeness returns. Tomas embraces and kisses her. Anna responds, but then stops and pushes him away with gentle firmness.

She stands with her head bowed and her hand on his shoulder . . . "No, not now, we have all the time in the world. Isn't it amazing?"

Many years ago, Mrs Borkman, wife of Councillor Borkman, had run a household with a great many servants, a great many guests, numerous relatives, a smaller number of prominent friends and some well-brought-up hangers-on. The dimensions of the kitchen accord with this. Everything seems to be in a sumptuous plural except the mighty stove. But otherwise . . . larders, ice-boxes, sinks, gas meters, kitchen clocks, food lifts, signalling devices, speaking tubes, serving tables, food tables, oil lamps, baking tables, preparation tables, high chairs, low chairs, stools, benches, curtainless windows facing the kitchen garden, an extensive scrubbed floor with no rugs, hot-water heater, cold-water pumps, garbage pails, glass cupboards filled with every kind of necessity, kitchen equipment, everyday china and Sunday porcelain, silver objects and ceramic vases.

They have laid the well-scrubbed long wooden table in the middle of the room, then eaten and drunk. They have lit some candles and are sitting opposite each other. The slim wine glasses have been filled, the bottles are on parade. One is empty . . . "Yes, Tomas, now your Anna is slightly tipsy and I'm telling you, *that* wasn't yesterday. I was born under the sign of Leo . . . and I'm really my mother's daughter and my mother, you see. Tomas, you aren't scared, are you? Are you afraid of me?"

"Sometimes, yes, sometimes I am."

"What is it that frightens you?"

"I don't know. I don't think like that."

"Oh, don't you? You don't think like that."

"I'm frightened when you . . ."

"When I take over?"

"Yes, something like that."

"Would you like some more wine?"

"Yes, please. It's nice."

"Yes, it's nice. Takes away tomorrow. For that matter, we'll never again make plans."

"Do you regret coming?"

"No. Yes, but not in the way you think."

"In what way?"

"I can't say."

She kisses his hand and holds it against his face, kisses it again and holds it to her forehead.

"Come now, my darling. Let's occupy Mrs Borkman's bedroom and Mrs Borkman's bed before our courage fails us."

Other rooms would certainly have been more suitable, but the fact was Märta had made up Mrs Borkman's bed in Mrs Borkman's thoughtfully warmed-up and cleaned bedroom. The certainly expensive wallpaper was of obscurely faded roses, the tiled stove a shimmering green tower crowned with shells and sinuous seagrass. The dark gleaming carved bed rose majestically in the middle of the room, a richly pleated canopy hovering above the four-poster's feather-bed and pillows. The pictures were of rural scenes, harvesting, mighty horses and boisterous children in national costumes. There was also a black-framed portrait of Councillor Borkman, deceased for decades, a corpulent man with iron-grey hair, bushy sidewhiskers and beard, large nose and commanding eyes. Orders of both foreign and native origins crowded on his well-tailored official suit. The embroidered velvet curtains over the high windows were drawn to hide the spring twilight.

The arched ceiling was moulded. Above the door to the little sitting-room and the somewhat smaller door to the ingenious dressing-room floated plaster cherubs entangled in garlands of flowers.

This mausoleum crammed with Mrs Borkman's prayers, disappointments, tears, suppressed passions and secret outbursts of rage, smelt of boiled cauliflower and something else that just might be identified as long since mummified rats. At the same time there was a faint smell of her heavy perfume of musk and rose-petals.

Anna stops on the threshold and laughs again. "No, no, it can't be true. Tomas! What do you say now?" She claps her hands, puts her arm round Tomas's waist and pushes him through the doorway. "But we must have some light."

She finds the curtain cord and the room is filled with the gentle night light – the light of a May night. The room is enlarged and flows out into dark shadows and suddenly illuminated objects; a grandfather clock with gilt hands, two pillars in Ionian style painted all over with clinging forest flowers, a small marble statue of a naked girl crouching, her face upturned, a remote richly carved writing table, a Japanese screen, thin and transparent, a glazed cupboard full of bound books.

The lovers are now to sleep in this scenery. Two lovers whose experience of each other's bodies is limited to shy meetings on a bed in a dirty student room. They have still not yet seen each other's nakedness apart from through the obscene candour of wet bathing costumes in sun and wind. They have embraced each other with eagerness, kissed each other's lips raw, they have fumbled inwards towards each other's secrets, brief moments on the borders of resignation. Everything has been closed eyes, fumblingly over and done with, summarily. Their shyness makes them diffident, for their bodies have never learnt a common language.

So prompting is up to Anna! "Now let's undress separately. I'll undress in the dressing-room and you undress in the sitting-room. But don't turn on the light. The window faces the road and someone might walk past and wonder what Mrs Borkman is up to in her old age." "Yes, let's do that," Tomas says, nodding with relief that Anna has taken the initiative.

Anna undresses in the yellow light of a lone light bulb in the shape of a lily-of-the-valley. It hangs high up and far away in Mrs Borkman's dressing-room. The narrow mirror on the door shows her from top to toe. She has loosened her hair and it falls down her shoulders and back as far as her waist. The white lace-edged underclothes glow in the dull light, her knee-length pantaloons with their ribbons at the thighs and broad elastic at the waist, the strictly tailored bodice which she unbuttons button by button after loosening the suspenders with unpretentious buttons in the long dark silk stockings. Her bodice is edged with wide lace and is slightly curved in towards the waist and ends with an embroidered border half-way down the thigh. Now she is naked apart from jewellery, wedding rings, the medallion on its gold chain and the small diamond ear-rings. Now she is naked, the young shapely body sharply outlined in the reflection from the ceiling light in the mirror. The slim arms, wrists, the smooth round thighs and stomach with its stretch marks from three deliveries. The inspection is objective but emotional. It's a question of not being attacked by the sickness of unreality. "Nightgown," she says clearly and pulls on a flannel nightgown with no orna-mentation at all. A deliberate choice. Chastity and natural cleanliness over a soul which is raging. "Don't think, maybe go to the w.c." Yes, she must. Mrs Borkman's water closet is on a small platform along the short wall of the dressing-room, hand rails of polished brass on each side.

Tomas has undressed and is sitting on the very edge of one of the silk-covered chairs in the little sitting-room. A boy's body, broad shoulders, sinewy arms, high chest, flat stomach, hairless apart from his sex, which is surrounded by a reddish bush of hair, slim haunches and long legs. His feet are small with neat toes. His right hip is a little bonier than the left from a childhood paralysis. He has combed his hair with a neat parting and has lit his pipe to calm himself. But he is not calm. The problem is that his nightshirt is in his suitcase and the suitcase is on a chair in the bedroom. He can't go into the bedroom naked, nor wearing long underpants with or without a shirt. If Anna saw him in such garb, the remaining magic of the white wine would evaporate and everything would be trivialised. Nor can he rush in and with two swift leaps hop into bed and thus conceal his nakedness under the feather-bed. That would be inconsistent with Anna's instructions. He considers getting dressed again, going in to fetch the night-shirt, apologising to Anna, going out again, undressing and putting on his nightshirt. An action of that kind would also ruin the sensitive atmosphere.

Anna has sat down on the bulging bed. She is brushing her long hair as if aimlessly and she calls out quietly to Tomas. He at once opens the door and goes in barefoot, but wearing his long well buttoned-up coat.

Anna and Tomas are helpless, defenceless. Both inwardly against themselves and outwardly against the majestic bed, the overloaded room, the exhausting sense of guilt forcefully tucked away. All this has to be overcome by the gestures and words of love. They have set out on a risky journey. Mysterious forces have been in movement. And now, at this moment, they find themselves at the terminus: she sitting on the high bed in her simple nightgown with her hairbrush in her right hand and he standing inside the door, barefoot, concealed by his shabby winter coat.

The room is lit by three sources of light, the inextinguishable spring twilight beyond the thin inner curtains over the window, the sleepy ceiling light and the flaring candle on the bedside table to the left of the bed. She is perhaps overcoming a tremor in her voice and tells him to take off his coat and that they are now to creep down into the bed and put their arms round each other. He obeys and turns out the ceiling light. She blows out the candle on the bedside table and there they are, under the feather-bed, their arms round each other, perhaps not altogether comfortable, but they have their arms round each other and he touches her hair. Breathing is sure to be difficult and the distance between them a chasm. But the light is unmoving beyond the lace curtains in the window. So as long as they don't close their eyes in terror, they can see each other quite clearly, and Tomas asks Anna to look at him – "We must look at each other, Anna." She has pressed her face to his shoulder. She tries to look at him. Difficult . . .

They fall asleep from exhaustion of the soul and the unreleased torment of their bodies.

Then it starts raining again, calmingly, good-naturedly. They fall asleep without coming any closer to each other. There is plenty of reason for compassion. The rôles they have allotted themselves and each other are not possible to perform, their only luggage the icy comments of their consciences, the presence of the sense of sin, their guilt over people close to them. And perhaps the most terrible of all, over that humiliated God. They have nothing to erect against that – they are defenceless.

They sleep for a few hours and it goes on raining. Darkness falls outside, and thus inside. He wakes and seeks her, and she pretends to be still asleep with her arms round his back. She parts her lips for a kiss, but the kiss is not forthcoming, his head falls back on the pillow and he is breathing heavily. She lets him lie like that, not disturbing him. There is nothing to say, as they lack words . . . that must come later . . . brilliant words from fiction, as all this has necessarily to be magnificently and uniquely transcendental. She thinks perhaps she ought to heave off that hot heavy body pressing her down into the soft bed . . . ought to wash. But she can't bring herself to disturb him, perhaps wake him. She remains unmoving, breathing quietly, her arms round him.

Tomas is sleeping like a child, soundly and quite silently, his mouth open. He smells of sleep and gastric catarrh. She is both warm and cold, and also needs to go to the w.c., and in addition, a sticky mess is running between her thighs and the smell of sperm revolts her. But she doesn't dare move, not at this moment. She forces the moment to remain as protection against the rusty knife of disappointment.

What is there to add except the dawn rain, the silence (not even a bird) and the smell of this alien room.

"Tomas."

"Yes."

"I want to get up."

"Of course."

"Move a little."

She sits up and pulls back her rumpled hair with both hands, her forehead hot, her cheeks hot, but she feels cold. Tomas is breathing deeply.

"I think I'm still asleep."

There is nothing to say to that. Anna touches the slumberer's face and shoulder. Then she gets up and opens the door to the now chilly Borkman bathroom.

Once more or less restored, she goes back, and Tomas isn't there. She crawls down into the feather-bed. No, she doesn't feel well and a cold shiver rises from her stomach, moving upwards. Her teeth are chattering. She's probably got a temperature.

She closes her eyes, but at once opens them again; she has presumably slept. Tomas is sitting on a chair by the door, fully dressed. His face is as white as paper and there are tears in his eyes.

"I'm leaving. The boat to Åndalnäs leaves in two hours, at seven o'clock. It departs an hour later on Sunday mornings. I'll walk to the harbour. It's not far. I found a tourist pamphlet down in the hall listing the arrivals and departures of the steamers. The *Otterøy* leaves at seven on Sundays. That's an hour later than on weekdays. Then I can catch the train. It leaves at five in the afternoon. It's a slow train . . . a passenger train which stops at every station. I won't be in Oslo until early Monday morning. Then there are several connections to choose from, but I can be in Stockholm by seven on Monday evening, then be in Upsala by nine at the latest."

Anna is sitting up in bed, her knees drawn up. She is burning hot now, has thrown the feather-bed to one side and pulled on her roomy nightgown. Her eyes are closed, her cheeks hot.

"Don't go."

"One has to be true."

She gasps and stares at him."What do you mean?"

"Well," says Tomas. "I mean exactly what I say. I have to be true, to myself. I realise to my horror that I haven't been true."

"In what way haven't you been true?" says Anna. She has hardly any voice.

"I ought to have seen my inadequacy. I ought to have told you that this whole trip was a mistake. Not for you, perhaps, but for me. I can't cope with breaking out. I am too . . . grey. I really knew all this from the start, but you took over, I was cowardly and didn't want to upset you, but I knew I was inadequate. I've always known that."

Tears come into his eyes, but he swallows them, sniffs helplessly and runs his hand over his face.

Anna has thought hard. This is serious, and now it's important that words and tone of voice agree.

"Please don't be so unhappy. Or let's at least be unhappy together. It's true we've launched into something that is too great and too dangerous. If we stay together, we can repair the damage."

She is eager now, her feverish shivering gone. She quickly gets out of bed and stands in front of him on the seagrass-patterned rug.

"What small feet you have," mumbles Tomas.

Early next morning, on May the twenty-sixth, Märta Gärdsjö returns to Molde on the night boat from Trondheim. She at once goes to the Borkman house to see that everything is in order and the two lovers have not left any compromising traces.

The weather has changed, the rain clouds and damp mist blown away and the morning is sunnily still. Even more fruit trees are in bloom in the old garden. Märta has not even been able to wait to take the bus, but has hired a cab.

When she goes in through the kitchen door, everything is apparently in perfect order, clean and tidy. She goes out into the spacious hall, hangs up her uniform coat and carefully removes her deaconess's starched cap. She smooths down her dark-brown hair, puts the little overnight bag down on a chair and turns towards the drawing-room, which is ablaze with the bright spring light.

Anna is standing in the doorway, her hand on the doorpost, her eyes swollen from crying and being up all night. Her hair has been carelessly done. She has her coat on, under it a glimpse of her shantung blouse and dark-blue skirt, a clearly visible stain on it just above the knee.

Märta can't stop herself, but the surprise in her voice rushes ahead of consideration and she says something like: "Oh, Anna! Are you *still here?* I thought you left early yesterday." Then she abruptly falls silent, takes a few steps and embraces Anna, who allows herself to be embraced, closes her eyes, her arms falling down her sides, then they both sink to the floor. They say nothing, no tears or explanations. Märta holds the devastated creature in her arms and they sit close together on the bare parquet floor in the sharp chequered pattern of sunlight. Eventually, Märta asks . . . extremely cautiously, whether Anna has telephoned her mother to tell her she has been delayed. Anna nods faintly. Yes, she has phoned, she phoned early on Monday morning.

After this explanation, spoken in a flat toneless voice, nothing is said for a long spell. Finally, Märta suggests that Anna should lie down for a while, and she is sure to need a cup of tea. Anna replies that she's cold and allows herself to be led to a sofa. She falls on to it, her head turned away and her arm over her face. Märta spreads Mrs Borkman's plaid rug over her. Anna doesn't answer the question about something to drink. She has fallen asleep.

Over the next few hours, Märta busies herself somewhere near the sleeping Anna. She puts a cup of herb tea laced with honey on the chair by her head. She hastily inspects the upper floor and the bedroom. Everything has been thoroughly cleaned and tidied and there's no trace of movements or emotions in the extensive semi-dark rooms. Anna's suitcases are packed and standing by the door. Her hat has been taken off the shelf. She has clearly been prepared to leave, but then hasn't been able to.

At three in the afternoon of the Tuesday, Anna wakes up and, staggering a trifle, makes her way to the cloakroom and spends a long time relieving herself. Then she washes her face in cold water, drinks Märta's tea, sitting upright like a sick little girl who has decided simply to adjust to all instructions. Märta has been in the library reading a fat volume containing two novels by Bjørnstjerne Bjørnson. When she notices that Anna has woken, she closes the book, puts it back on the shelf and goes into the drawing-room, where she sits down on a chair by the window. The sunlight has now moved to the south-west side of the house, leaving the long heavily furnished room in the half light.

Anna is drinking her tea, still in her overcoat.

Her friend watches and waits.

Anna carefully puts the cup back on the chair and wipes her mouth with the back of her hand. Then she sinks back in the soft sofa, kicks off her embroidered slippers and pulls the plaid rug round her.

"Are you still cold?"

"No, no, I'm fine."

"Would you like some more tea?"

"No, thank you."

"How are you feeling?"

"All right, I think. I've got slight toothache, I think."

"You've slept for six hours."

"What's the time?"

"Nearly half past three."

Märta consults the little gold watch she keeps on a thin gold chain in the top pocket of her uniform.

"I took some bromide powders I found in Mrs Borkman's bedside table. That was last night, I think. But then I couldn't sleep after all. I walked around most of the night. Then I was suddenly horribly sick and got that stain on my skirt. I tried to get it out, but couldn't. And then I just stayed sitting."

"Have you got another skirt?"

"Yes, probably."

They seem to have run out of subjects of conversation, but Märta waits patiently. Anna yawns and closes her eyes.

"Tomas wanted to go for a walk early on Sunday morning. He said he wanted to be alone for a while. He went off down to the harbour and found out that the mail boat left for Åndalsnäs in the afternoon. He came back at once and told me he was leaving. He borrowed a hundred kronor and left. I stayed behind."

Anna laughs quietly, turns her head away and draws a deep breath.

"What did you do?"

"That was on Sunday, and you tell me it's now Tuesday. I don't know. Everything's floated together. I mostly walked round the rooms. That in itself was interesting."

"So you're going home early tomorrow morning?"

"What? Yes. Going home? I don't know. Yes, perhaps."

"Of course you are. I'll go with you if you like. To make sure you get on the right train and so on."

"How you do arrange things and decide."

"Mr Egerman has forgotten his scores."

"We'd planned he would play in the church, so he brought some scores with him. Nothing came of it. Oh, how it hurts."

"You hurt?"

"Yes, my tooth. I went to the dentist the day before I came here, and he cleared it all up. Have you got any pain-killers, or anything?"

"Yes, in my bag. Wait a moment and I'll get them. I think I put my bag in the hall, yes, that's it. There it is. Now, let's see. I'm sure I . . . here's the box. I *knew* I had some. There, take it with a mouthful of tea. There's some left in the cup. That's it."

Anna grasps Märta's hand and presses it against her cheek. She mumbles something about things being all right, all right because I have a friend who is kind and doesn't ask questions.

"Then we're agreed we'll leave early tomorrow morning."

"One thing I really do know."

"What's that?"

"I know that I did Tomas a great wrong by making him come here."

"He probably couldn't say no."

"How could that have happened? I was so eager. No, no, no. He probably made some objections. Small ones, quiet objections."

Her laugh again, quiet and strange. She has curled up in the bulging sofa with its white summer cover and is leaning her head against the richly embroidered cushion. Mrs Borkman's fluffy plaid rug pulled right up to her chin. Märta has sat down on the same sofa and has her hand on the hump that is Anna's foot under the rug.

"The worst of it is, the very worst . . ."

"Yes."

"Do you know what was so terrible?"

"No."

"I saw *Henrik's* face. Have you ever considered that peculiar phenomenon when you can't remember faces you see every day? I try to recall my mother's face . . . or yours, or the children's . . . but I can't. If I'm dreaming, I *know* I'm dreaming about someone close to me, someone I see every day. The dream tells me that is so . . . though the face is seldom the right face, but an unknown one. But suddenly, when I was walking around here . . . it must have been on Sunday evening because it had started to be . . . no, it was probably Monday evening . . . or was it . . .? I don't know. But suddenly I saw Henrik's face. It hurt dreadfully, because it wasn't at all Henrik as he looks today. Not that face which is autocratic or malicious or weeping, or that Henrik complaining, or anguished. Not that mask of a face. Not Henrik when he is being demanding, or frightening or just stupid. It was another face, and despite everything it wasn't at all the Henrik I loved many years ago when we were young. The appealing, gentle, happy, uncertain, loving, kindly face. Not *that* Henrik. No, I saw an elderly face . . . an old Henrik. He was eighty or thereabouts. I kept seeing him over and over again, not in front of me, not as some kind of ghost or anything like that. No, I saw him at the back of my eyes. The image was quite tangible and kept coming back, and it hurt. I wanted to whimper and complain, but nothing came of that. I just kept seeing it and it was almost unbearable. There was so much grief and vulnerability and determination in Henrik's face, and now I know *he is the elderly child.* And I was the one given him as my lot. And then I think that it is inscribed in my rôle in life that I am to inflict on him wounds that never heal. Infected wounds . . . the ones that do the most harm, that are never inflamed, which never heal. And he clings on tightly and I am frightened and furious, and when he seriously threatens my wretched freedom, I mortally wound him. I could easily kill him. And the weapon is Tomas."

Anna is calm, speaking calmly. The eye of the storm. The time like in dreams.

"And Tomas?"

"Tomas has left me, but I won't leave him."

Her head sinks down against the embroidered cushion and she pulls the plaid rug up round her shoulders. "I'm going out to the kitchen to see what there is for dinner," says Märta dryly, and leaves the room.

Anna's grandfather's ring is lying on the little table by the sofa.

Fifth conversation
October 1934

It is eleven o'clock in the morning on Sunday, October the fourteenth, 1934. The place is Upsala, beyond the corner between Upper Slottsgatan and Skolgatan. It has been raining all morning, an icy wind blowing in from the plain and predicting snow. At the moment, the clouds have dispersed and low, thinly veiled sunlight is streaming in over Gustavianum, the thunder of the bells of the Cathedral and Holy Trinity church summoning to morning service. The streets are empty.

The taxi cab stops by the entrance to number fourteen Skolgatan. Anna gets out, opens her handbag and takes out the little chamois-leather purse with its silvered clasp. She pays one krona and ten öre, then adds a twenty-five öre tip. The driver, a red-faced man with a drooping moustache, nods silently, changes gear and disappears in a cloud of smoke.

Anna stays standing in thought for a moment. She is forty-five, her face scarcely changed, her lips a little thicker, softer, her nose slightly red from the wind. Her eyes are grave; they express searching curiosity. There is a long horizontal scratch on her forehead. Otherwise, she is upright and neat in her warm winter coat, black hat, gloves and bootees.

She looks at her wristwatch with a swift habitual glance, although she knows perfectly well it's five past eleven, because the bells have just stopped ringing. She has come too early, but after a short walk along Slottsgatan, she decides to go in anyhow and she opens the big entrance gate with some

96

difficulty. The stairwell with its stained-glass windows is a fair size, the marble treads carpeted, and there is an ornamental entrance to the back courtyard. Huge copper lamps with engraved glass globes hang from the *art-nouveau* painted ceiling. There is a smell of new paint and then breakfast.

Anna quickly mounts the two flights of stairs and rings the bell on the glass-fronted white double doors on that floor. A tall thin woman opens the door, a woman in her seventies with lively greyish-blue eyes, high forehead, slim shapely nose, thin lips and rather baggy pale cheeks. Her hair is thin and drawn back into an unpretentious knot. So this is Maria.

"Oh, Anna, how nice, already here! Come on in, come in. How lovely to see you, beautiful as ever. Here's a hanger. Wait, I'll hang it up. Give me a kiss."

Anna has mumbled some excuse for her early arrival, and returned the welcoming kiss, certainly with great affection. She has sat down on a white basket chair, taken off her overshoes and put them on the shoe-shelf below the coat rack, Then she smooths down her unruly hair and takes her powder compact out of her bag. After blowing her nose with small trumpeting sounds, she powders it with great care.

"The moment there's a touch of autumn, my nose gets large and red. It's been like that ever since I was a child."

Inspection and relative satisfaction. She is wearing a dark-blue woollen dress with buttons on the skirt. It comes down to her calves and the wide sleeves end in lace cuffs, the collar circular and also edged with lace. In addition, a cameo at her throat and small diamond ear-rings.

"Jacob's having a little sleep. Dr Petréus came this morning and gave him a morphine injection. So he'll sleep for an hour or so now."

"How is he?"

"The doctor says it's near the end now, only a matter of days. It's difficult sometimes. He has a lot of pain and then the morphine is the only thing that helps. In between he's relatively all right and can even eat something, but he mostly just has a glass of milk or some bouillon – or champagne."

Maria smiles quickly and gestures with her big thin hand.

"You mustn't be horrified. This isn't a house of mourning. There are torments and physical humiliations, and some impatience because death takes its time. But we're not grieving. Neither I nor Jacob."

"Are you sure he can be bothered to see me, Maria?"

"He's talked about you every day. Otherwise, I wouldn't have phoned, do you see?"

"Henrik sends his regards. He couldn't come because of morning service."

"Well, you see, Anna, that was intended. Jacob asked to find out when Henrik was taking morning service and then . . ."

She smiles conspiratorially, reaches for a silver box on the round drawing-room table, takes out a cigarette and lights it immediately.

"I didn't offer you one. I remember that you don't smoke. I hope you don't mind."

Anna shakes her head and smiles politely. Maria leans back in the little green upholstered armchair. With a characteristic gesture, she puts her right hand to the small of her back and holds the cigarette in left hand just in front of her lips.

"We had a bad day last Friday. His stomach had swollen until it was grotesque. Dr Petréus drained off a whole mass of fluid. That was a relief, anyhow. But all the same, the worst of it was that he kept vomiting bile. It comes in waves and is terrible . . . the doctor and the nurse and I . . . there's nothing we can do, not morphine, nothing. He has metastases everywhere now, as if the cancer were racing through him."

She falls silent and gazes at the ceiling. Then she looks at Anna, her large grey-blue eyes clear and steady. Her face is pale in the harsh October light with its streaks of sharp light and dark, the low October sun. No, she's not crying.

"We've lived close to each other for almost fifty years. I was twenty-one when we married. Should it come about that we were able to see each other again after death, if such a mysterious possibility exists, then all these ... externals would probably be easier to bear. And death would be a relief, as Jacob would be released from his torments and I from a burdensome waiting. But death is death. No mysteries or beautiful secrets. Do you know, for that matter, what's so remarkable, a consoling thought that comes to me when I'm tormented by distress? Well, the separation would be much more painful if our marriage had not been good. We've been allowed to live with joy and then . . ."

She smokes in silence, then presses the remains of the cigarette into a small ashtray and gets up briskly, smoothing her skirt down over her angular hips.

"It was kind of you to listen. I'm not really given to talking like this, I'll have you know. I'll go in to Jacob now and see if he's awake."

At the door, she turns round and now she is speaking as if in passing.

"I forgot to tell you that Dean Agrell is coming this afternoon. Jacob wanted him to give him communion. He was to be here at about one. I'll come and fetch you in a minute or two."

The library, a spacious square room with two windows facing Upper Slottsgatan; it is lined with bookcases, and there is a bulky heaped desk in the middle of the floor. A narrow doorway leads into an inner room where a high-ended bed can just be seen. A high-backed chair with strong arms is by the library table, Jacob seated in it, his neat suit sagging round his emaciated figure. The stiff white collar is several sizes too large, the hands resting on the arms of the chair large and without strength, the wrists encircled by far too roomy cuffs. But the knot of his tie is irreproachable, his high boots polished and his grey moustache trimmed. There is no sign of approaching death about the old man.

Anna kisses him on the cheek and embraces both him and the chair, both of them moved and slightly clumsy. Jacob touches her hair with his big hand and pulls her head to his shoulder.

"Anna, my dear, how nice. Dear Anna. You're just the same. Dear Anna."

"It's been a long time. It must be a long time since?"

"Yes, wait a minute, let me see. We met in Hedvig Leonora church two ... no, it's actually three years ago. Henrik was preaching. It must have been the Sunday before Advent in 1932, and you were there, Anna, with the children and a little German boy, isn't that right?"

"Yes, Helmuth."

"Geographically we become far away from each other even if the distance isn't so great. Geographically ... yes. But not, how shall I put it? Not so that it matters. Not in your feelings. I often think about you, Anna."

"And I think about ..."

They look closely at each other, so close that they can see only a small part of face and eye. On a sudden impulse, Anna runs her hand over Jacob's forehead.

"I mustn't complain. I'm all right in my wretchedness. But that it should take so long. He dawdles, he does, that one. Serves me right, because I've always been both impatient and lazy. Now I have to make an effort. Hour by hour, minute by minute. And I ... But I want to be up and dressed. I want to sit in my chair as often as I can. I can breathe more easily then. Though it's difficult sometimes, here among all my old books. Maria has to open the window and let in fresh air, you see, Anna. But I have a strong heart. It goes on and on. One evening my heart started galloping, then it stopped and had second thoughts, and then I thought that ... *now!* But no. So I've become a morphine addict. That's the best of all this long miserable story. If you think I seem too cheerful and talkative, Anna, that's because I've just had an injection and that's like paradise ... I can't imagine anything more full of grace. First pain and misery and then no pain and euphoria. So it's a question of dividing the time between good and evil. Maria reads aloud to me for several hours a day ... I'm too tired and muddle-headed to be able to read. But we're reading *The Queen's Jewel*. Sometimes the cathedral organist – what's his name? – comes. You can see, Anna, I've become rather confused. Yes ... Axel. Axel Morath. He comes and plays on the piano out there in the drawing-room and then it's Bach, *Wohltemperirte Klavier*, mostly. Though I've no need for company. That's tiring and trouble-some. Friends think you want to be visited, but you don't. So Maria keeps saying no. There's only one *really* tedious thing in all this tedium and that's that I can't eat. I can only take a little fluid and that's dreadful. When I think what a glutton and voluptuary I used to be. Guzzling, helping myself and drinking deeply. Sometimes when I'm on my own (and haven't too much pain, of course), I imagine various dishes. Yes, it's probably a punishment, I suppose. Gluttony is one of the seven deadly sins. How are things with you, Anna? How are things?"

The question comes abruptly, spoken in a stern tone of voice, followed by a quizzical look. Go ahead. Now we've got to the point. Anna is uncertain, surprised and flushing.

"What do you mean, Uncle Jacob?"

"I mean what I say and nothing else. *How are things?*

His tone of voice is impatient and will accept no evasions. Answer immediately, please. Anna hesitates, affected by a brief shadowy anger, and replies that "things are nothing special, much as usual. It would be ungrateful to complain. Yes, and the children are well. Mamma has had pneumonia but is recovering. And Henrik is very tense over the church appoint-ment ... but you know that, Uncle Jacob. The government decision has been delayed. Engberg has nothing against it, but the old king is said to want to have Henrik, and so the appointment has been allowed to lie on the table, as they say. And that's a strain on the nerves."

The old man makes a gesture of impatience, running his hand over his face, smiling sarcastically and clearing his throat.

"I didn't ask for a communiqué. I wanted to know what your life's like, Anna, what Henrik's is like, what came of it all. We haven't talked seriously for ten years. So the time has come. I read somewhere that Tomas has married and I heard he'd been given a living out on the Upsala plain."

"Yes, I heard that, too."

"Now you're being taciturn, Anna. Aren't I worthy of being told what became of it all?"

"Well, it's just that I don't know whether there's anything to tell."

"The reason why I asked Maria to get in touch with you, the reason was that I didn't want to go to my grave without knowing how things had worked out. I have always regarded you as my child, Anna, my daughter. A day doesn't go by when I don't think about your life. I have noted that your marriage hasn't fallen apart. Many a time I've thought I should talk to you, Anna. But I'm a lazy and unenterprising kind of person who likes to postpone everything that disturbs my peace, so I put it off as usual, and suddenly everything was long ago. Though now . . . In the long hours of my illness, our conversation has come back to me and given me no peace. In the end I asked Maria to seek you out. And now, Anna, now we're *face to face*. Now the time has come."

The old man has been speaking quickly and eagerly, but suddenly he is tired and turns his head away, so that Anna can't see his eyes. She runs her beringed left hand over the smooth dark-blue of her skirt.

When the silence has gone on too long, the old man turns his eyes on Anna and looks at her challengingly. I want to know now.

"Well." Then Anna lies, quietly and with no special

emphasis. "I did as you advised me, Uncle Jacob. When I went out to the summer place the next evening, it seemed appropriate, as Henrik and I were alone there. I told him precisely what the situation was. I didn't leave anything out. Not even the most painful parts. Henrik listened without interrupting, looking at me all the time but saying nothing. Then when I had finished telling him, we were silent for a long time. Then we began to talk to each other and I dared to tell him more about myself than ever before in all the twelve years we had lived together. It was an amazing evening, and I thought about what you had said about giving Henrik the chance to mature. No reproaches, no threats, no bitterness. Nothing bad."

"You see, Anna! You see?"

"Yes, I see."

"And then?"

Anna reflects. The beringed hand runs over the dark-blue of her skirt.

"I did as you advised me. I broke with Tomas. It was difficult, but after I'd told Henrik everything, that secretive existence couldn't go on. So I broke with Tomas. There were tears, of course. But now it's all a beautiful memory . . . and Tomas has married. Well, you know that. I never see him."

"And Henrik overworking?"

"He works tremendously hard. He always works tremendously hard. He can't say no when people ask him. And that year was hard in many ways. The children were ill. I was ill, too. Then came Henrik's breakdown. Well, you know all that, Uncle Jacob. I didn't try to influence him. I just waited. When Henrik was to start work again, naturally there were problems. After that, there's nothing much to tell. I had two operations and nearly died. Mamma came to the rescue and looked after our household. It probably wasn't all that easy . . . Henrik and Ma have never really seen eye to eye . . . though that's calmed down over the years . . . but their animosity is a burden . . . I can't deny that."

"But Anna and Henrik?"

"Anna and Henrik are good friends. We can even quarrel without troublesome consequences . . . we could never do that before. Henrik realises that I need a little freedom, only a little. So next summer, I and two other women are thinking of going to Italy to visit the museums."

Jacob draws a deep breath and closes his eyes. He smiles faintly.

"To be honest, I was worried. But I never dared ask. What you've told me, Anna, is a great relief to me. I say like old Simeon in the Temple: Now, oh Lord, let thy servant go in peace according to thy word."

He pulls Anna to him and kisses her clumsily by the ear, his lips tightly closed. A dry sob escapes him.

"Forgive me, but I may well smell a little. I feel great love for your courage, Anna. Do you remember when we stood down by the Cathedral Bridge and counted Upsala's seven bridges?"

"Yes."

Anna is seized with a surge of emotion. She carefully extricates herself and goes over to the window, wipes her eyes with the back of her hand and sniffs, no, don't cry now, don't cry.

Maria comes silently into the room and goes over to her husband. They confer in whispers. "Yes, we'll do that," says Jacob in a clear voice.

"Anna, would you wait outside for a few minutes. We'll soon be ready."

Anna says yes, of course, and goes quietly out, closing the door, then finds herself suddenly facing Dean Agrell in his full priestly garb. He is a few years older than Jacob, but his reddish face radiates good health, his thinning white hair wispy and brushed back from his wrinkled brow. His eyes are icy blue and inquisitively observant.

"I happen to be one of Jacob's oldest friends. He has asked me to give him communion, now, today, the anniversary of our ordination fifty years ago."

Maria opens the door a little and says it's all right to come in now. She opens the door wide and lets the dean in. Then she comes out, closes the door and stands there rather irresolutely.

"Jacob wanted them to be alone together for a few minutes."

A small gesture and an apologetic look. "Are you staying, Anna?"

"Yes."

"I think Jacob'll be pleased you . . ."

"Yes."

"I remember that evening long ago, 1907, I think, when Jacob came in and sat on the edge of my bed and said, what do you think, Maria. Anna Åkerblom says she doesn't want to go to communion. He couldn't sleep that night. He was both surprised and annoyed, and truly sad. Then you went after all."

"Yes, I did, yes."

"And the reason? I'm only curious."

"The reason was simple. When I told Mamma I wasn't going to communion, she was really angry and said I ought to be ashamed, that I was selfish and spoilt and it would be an affront to the family and she had no intention of tolerating such foolishness. Before Mamma slammed the door, she turned round and said she was thinking of cancelling our trip to Greece, but naturally I had my own free will and that as usual I would do what my conscience told me and no one would make me. So I went to communion."

Both women smile at the thought of Anna's mother, the determined but nowadays fragile old lady over there in the big apartment house in Trädgårdsgatan.

"Give my love to Karin, Anna. Sadly, it's a long time since we last saw each other. But there's been so much illness and troubles recently."

"I'll tell her."

The door opens slightly and Maria holds out her long thin hand to Anna and together they go into the sick-room.

The low square table by Jacob's chair has been cleared and now has on it two lighted candles in pewter candlesticks. On an embroidered cloth is the gilded chalice with the wine and in front of that the similarly gilded dish of wafers. Dean Agrell is leaning over the sick man. They are conversing in whispers; the low sunlight pours dazzling rays through the room and draws irregular patterns on the treasures in the bookcases. The clock in the drawing-room has just struck one and the bells of Holy Trinity church are ringing.

The dean nods towards the two who have just come in and invites them to come closer – they have stopped inside the door. Maria turns to Anna and again holds out her hand to pull her to her. Anna lets it happen. The priest has placed himself in front of Jacob, who has closed his eyes, his big hands resting on the broad arms of the chair. He is deathly pale in the strong light, apparently preoccupied, but for the moment free of physical pain. He is sitting up straight, neat and collected. Maria smooths his hair down and brushes a few grains off dust of the shoulder of his jacket. She bends quickly down and whispers a few words in his great ear. He smiles almost imperceptibly and with his eyes still closed, he whispers something back.

Dean Agrell picks the prayer book up from the improvised altar, stands deep in thought for a moment, then reads the words of institution for communion in a very low voice, directed entirely at the sick man, enveloping him with his voice and mind. Maria looks at her clasped hands. She is collected, as if before a task of great importance that is approaching completion. Anna has turned her face to the harsh light, allowing herself to be dazzled, tears, restrained tears fastening in her throat and running down her nose, trying to breathe calmly, this can't be put into words, this is beyond formulated emotions. There are Jacob and his wife Maria, now. At this moment. If she turns her eyes away from the dazzling light between the house wall and the huge tree. She can't. But she knows.

Dean Agrell is standing reading the words of institution of communion.

"On the night the Lord Jesus was betrayed, he took bread, gave thanks to God, broke it and gave to his disciples and said: take and eat. This is my body, hallowed for you. Do this for my commemoration.

"Our Father which art in heaven, Hallowed be thy Name. Thy Kingdom come. Thy will be done, in earth as it is in heaven.

"Give us this day our daily bread. And forgive us our trespasses, As we forgive them that trespass against us.

"And lead us not into temptation, but deliver us from all evil.

"For thine is the kingdom, the power and the glory, for ever and ever, Amen."

Anna and Maria have knelt down and are also saying the prayer. With an effort, Jacob has clasped his hands . . . his eyes are still closed, his face calm but suddenly with dark shadows below his eyes. He moves his lips but no words can be distinguished.

The dean lifts the plate with the wafers and takes a step towards the sick man, leans over him. Jacob opens his lips.

"The Body of our Lord Jesus Christ, which was given for thee." The priest puts his hand on Jacob's head. Then he turns to Maria and hands her a wafer. She receives it, her face upturned.

"The Body of our Lord Jesus Christ, which was given for thee." He holds his hand over her thin grey hair, now lit through by the sharp light. Finally he takes a step towards Anna, who shakes her head . . . no, no. Dean Agrell doesn't notice or refuses to accept Anna's dismissive gesture.

"The Body of our Lord Jesus Christ, which was given for thee." The wafer. The blessing by his hand. He doesn't look at her. No one is looking at her except herself. Weight, she wants to sink deep down to the floor. But she restrains herself.

The priest has now taken the chalice and puts it carefully to the sick man's lips.

"The Blood of our Lord Jesus Christ, which was shed for thee."

Then he turns to Maria, who accepts the means of grace with her face turned to the chalice.

"The Blood of our Lord Jesus Christ, which was shed for thee."

Finally Anna, finally Anna.

"The Blood of our Lord Jesus Christ, which was shed for thee."

Dean Agrell takes a step back and speaks to the assembled.

"Lord Jesus Christ, preserve thy body and soul unto everlasting life. Amen."

Jacob opens his eyes and looks at his colleague with a faint touch of a smile. "Don't forget the psalm."

"It's coming now."

Jacob again closes his eyes and the priest reads:

"Lastly, Almighty God, I thee now pray: take my hand in thine. So that thou always leadest. Take me to thy joyful land. Where all troubles end. And when hope is ended. And I thee my spirit send. Take it then . . ."

Jacob falls forward with a violent spasm. He tries to put his hands over his mouth, but out through his lips comes a yellowish blood-streaked fluid that trickles down his chin. At an even stronger spasm, his mouth opens and blood and mucus spurt out with a dull belch. He tries to get up from his chair, but falls back, gasping for breath. Anna takes his arm and holds it above his head, and his wife takes the other arm, but more grey viscous fluid spurts from his throat and down over his dark suit.

The attack subsides. It has lasted longer than a minute or so. Dean Agrell says quickly: "I think Sister Ellen is still here, perhaps she's waiting out there. Would you fetch her, Anna. She's sure to be somewhere in the apartment."

Anna runs through the drawing-room out into the hall. The door to the pantry is open and she sees Sister Ellen sitting in the kitchen with a cup of coffee and the Upsala paper in front of her. "Please come at once, Sister. The Reverend has been taken ill." Sister Ellen hurries away. Anna stands in the hall. She can hear voices and rapid footsteps. Water running in the bathroom, hissing in the pipes, a door shutting.

Epilogue–Prologue
May 1907

"So all of you confirmands will find yourselves before God himself – before the face of God. He receives anyone who flees to him. All those in need of forgiveness and wishing to live as his child are just those he wishes to see at communion. Dear friends, let us now read the Blessing together. Oh Lord, bless us and keep us; oh Lord let thy face shine over us and be merciful to us; oh Lord turn thy face to us and give us peace. In the name of the Father, the Son and the Holy Ghost. Amen."

This is being said one May evening in one of the side-chapels of the Cathedral, where Jacob has assembled his confirmation candidates before their first communion on the following day. Sixteen young people, four of them boys. The year is 1907 and one of the young women is Anna Åkerblom, now seventeen.

On the photograph that exists, she is sitting to the right of the Cathedral pastor. She is wearing her lovely confirmation dress, her head thrust slightly forward, and she is looking searchingly at me.

This evening, however, she is dressed in more ordinary clothes, checked blouse with wide half-length sleeves and broad lace collar held together with a silver brooch. Her skirt is of fine wool, dark-blue and pleated. On the third finger of her right hand she has a ring mounted with a small cameo. It is possible this young lady is no beauty, but she is visible without making too much fuss about it.

Jacob is forty-six, a tall man, broad, heavy, his hands large. He is enveloped in a cassock of irreproachable cut and noticeable neatness. His hair is light-brown and parted at the side, his eyes large and slightly protruding, his forehead high, the eyebrows thick and straight. His eyes are bright blue and his nose looms large, dominating his heavy straggly moustache, his chin broad and shapely. As I remember him, his voice was deep, with a trace of a country accent.

Now ... that is, in 1907 ... for several years, Jacob has been active in the archbishop's diocese and is expected to take the step to bishop within the not too distant future. I should add that for several years he has been a welcome visitor at the Åkerblom household in Trädgårdsgatan.

"We'll assemble in the parish room at half past ten. When the bell rings at a quarter to eleven, we shall all go in procession together into the Cathedral. I shall stop at the pew reserved for you and make sure you're in the right place. You will all have your prayer books with you. You may not receive flowers or gifts before the service. So, thank you, all of you, and we'll see each other again at our festival tomorrow. Good evening and goodnight to you all."

The pastor lowers his head for a moment and closes his eyes, then looks at his pupils with an absent-minded smile: you can go now. The boys and girls at once do as they are told, at first silently and gravely, then a few moments later, noisily and boisterously.

Mr Stille the verger materialises by the altar in the side-chapel, puts the chairs back into straight rows and picks a hymn book up off the floor. Jacob stays where he is for a moment, looking thoughtfully after his confirmation class.

"Terrible what a noise they make," says Mr Stille. "And here's a prayer book one of them's forgotten. Yes, yes, yes. There's a name in it, but I can't even read the writing. Samselius or something."

"If you're going over to the parish room anyhow, Mr Stille,

perhaps you'd be good enough to put it on the table by the window."

"Very well, Pastor."

"Then I'll get my coat. Goodnight, Mr Stille."

"Goodnight, Pastor."

Jacob goes briskly into the vestry, a large irregular room, its high vaulted ceiling disappearing above the sleepily glowing electric lights with their green shades. A row of glass cupboards along the walls contains the costumes and props for the church rituals, and in the middle of the floor is a pale oak table guarded by six chairs with high carved backs and worn leather seats. By the door is a narrow full-length mirror. The dark room is chilly and smells of lime, mould and the bones of the dead.

There are three doors, an arched one to the altar, a high narrow one with steps up to the pulpit and then the low wide doors into the north entrance of the church.

Anna is standing inside the double door. She has fetched her light spring overcoat and fastened her much too ladylike hat on with a long hatpin. She has her prayer book in her gloved hand. The Pastor has just put his coat on and taken his hat down from the rack, then sees her and stops.

"I'd like to talk to you, Uncle Jacob. If that's all right. If you have time, I mean. I won't be long."

"It'd be better if we could leave it until next week. I've all the time in the world on Wednesday."

"Then it'll be too late."

"Too late? What do you mean, Anna?"

"Can we sit down? Just for a few moments."

"Of course, of course. I must just tell Mr Stille he'll have to wait for a few minutes before putting the lights out and locking up."

Jacob disappears out into the church and can be heard talking to the verger . . . "No, no, of course, that's perfectly all right. I have things to do. Just tell me, Pastor. I'll be out there."

Jacob is back, puts his hat on the table and sits down on one of the high-backed chairs. Anna sits at the curved end of the table, the distance great. The brim of her hat shades her eyes, making her anonymous. She raises her arms, pulls out the gleaming hatpin and puts the hat down, smiling apologetically.

"It's a new hat. I thought it was elegant."

"Oh well, Anna, I expect you'll gradually grow into it. I'm sure it'll suit you."

The pastor is about to ask what it was Anna wanted, but stops and waits. The girl evidently has something on her mind and she is finding it hard to bring it out.

"Pappa sends his regards and hopes you will come to dinner next Sunday. As Aunt Maria is away on a cure, Pappa thought perhaps you might be feeling lonely."

"That was nice of him, but all the same, I'm not sure."

"The Aulin Quartet is performing in the main university hall on Sunday, at three o'clock, then they're all coming to dinner. Pappa said they are a nice lot and you at least know Tor Aulin and Rudolf Claesson. Then we were going to make music in the evening."

"Ah, that sounds tempting."

"Mamma will phone you. But that really wasn't at all . . ."

"I realise that."

Suspense. Anna pokes at a broken nail and tries to say something. Jacob goes on waiting, giving her time.

"It's a matter of some difficulty."

"I imagine so."

"And I'm afraid you'll be annoyed."

"I don't think anything you can say would annoy me, Anna."

Suspense. Anna smiles apologetically, tears coming into her eyes.

"Well, it's like this."

"Now, Anna, out with it."

The pastor is not told what the "this" is. But he refrains

from asking questions or making any attempt to wheedle it out of her.

"You see, it's like this. I don't want to take communion."

She takes her handkerchief out of her handbag and blows her nose.

"If you don't want to take communion, you must have a good reason, Anna."

"I'm trying to imagine myself kneeling at the altar rail and then the wafer and the wine . . . no. It would be a deception."

"Deception is a strong word."

"A lie, then, if that's any better. If I was to take part in that ritual, then I would be acting . . . I can't."

"I think we'll take a little walk. Let's go up to Odin's Grove and admire the spring."

Anna nods and smiles with embarrassment. Jacob holds the door open and they go out into the church. The twilight beyond the high windows gives rise to a mysterious infinity up into the arches and towards the organ loft. Mr Stille waves goodnight and closes the church door.

Walking slowly, they cross Biskopsgatan.

"Let's stop now. Are you cold? No? Then let's sit down on this bench. Did you know that Holy Trinity church was originally called Bondkyrka church after the parish called Bondkyrka. It was there in the twelfth century. So this is a good place to sit. We can talk about eternal questions in the shelter of eternity."

"Are you a believer, Uncle Jacob?"

"I think I can answer yes to that question. I can also tell you the actual reason . . . a factual circumstance that can never be contradicted, not even by the sharpest doubter. Do you want to hear it?"

"Yes."

"Well. When Jesus Christ was executed by crucifixion, he was taken out of the world. He didn't exist any more. The scriptures do indeed discuss the empty tomb, the angel who spoke to the two women. There's also the story that Mary Magdalene had met Jesus and talked to him, and that the Master visited his Apostles and let Thomas the Doubter touch his wounds. All that's evangelical testimony, stories for consolation and joy. But nothing to do with the decisive miracle."

"The miracle?"

"Yes, Anna. The miracle, the unfathomable. Think about the Apostles, who had fled in all directions like frightened rabbits. Peter had denied Jesus. Judas had betrayed him. Everything was at an end, gone. A few weeks after the disaster, they met in a secret place. They were frightened and shattered. Their failure is a painful fact. All their dreams of creating together with the Messiah the new kingdom are crushed. They are humiliated and ashamed. They find it hard to look each other in the eyes. They talk of fleeing, of emigration, of apologising in the synagogues and to the priests. That is when the miracle occurs ... as incomprehensible as it is magnificent."

Jacob pauses slightly ... a small artificial pause, perhaps to test out his audience's interest. There is no one anywhere near them. The long flowerbeds of Odin's Grove and the fresh leaves of the elms give off waves of heavy fragrance. The little tram makes its laborious way up the slope past Gustavianum, screeching on the corner and sliding into Biskopsgatan, to disappear silently down by Trädgårdsgatan, its windows glowing faintly. It looks like a gliding blue lantern.

"The miracle?"

"Yes, yes, the miracle. The most credible, the simplest but also the most magnificent of all the evangelists' miracles. You can see the Apostles sitting there in the long darkening room. They have perhaps eaten a simple evening meal together, which has perhaps reminded them of their last meal with their Master. But now they are despondent, despairing, and, as I said ... literally mortal afraid. Then Peter gets to his feet, the one who denied Jesus ... and stands before his friends, saying nothing. They look at him in astonishment ... is he going to say something? He is certainly not known as an orator, and since the disaster, he has been more silent than ever. None the less, now he is standing there, about to say something, stammering and uncertain, though soon with greater and greater eagerness. He says now there must be an end to this time of cowardice and shame. Haven't he and his friends been for nine months part of the most amazing thing that has happened to anyone since the beginning of time? They have listened to the message of invincible love. The Master has looked at them and they have turned their faces towards him. They have listened and understood. They have realised they were chosen. For nine months they have lived enveloped in a new insight and an unfathomable solicitude. And what do they do? asks Peter, looking round in anger. Yes, they return the Master's gift by hiding in their holes like mangy rats. The hours and days and weeks go by, says Peter. 'And we spend our time ... this priceless time sustaining our wretched lives to no useful purpose. And now I ask,' says Peter, 'now I ask whether the time has not come to turn right round. For nothing can be more wretched than our present lives, or lack of life. Why are we driven into the darkness and this cowardice, when we can go out into the light and tell everyone ... as many people as possible before we're caught, tortured and killed ... tell them that love exists like the disregarded reality in our lives? We have no choice, if we don't choose to die of suffocation in our holes? Think on this: a short while ago, the Master walked past us by chance and *saw us and called us by name* and ordered us to follow him. He chose us, one by one and all together, because he knew or thought he knew we would carry his message on.'

"Peter looked at each one of his friends and spoke to them by name. They were eleven in number, as Judas had hanged himself, he, who was perhaps the most devoted and took revenge because he thought he had been betrayed. 'Do you remember what the Master said to us when he called us? Follow me and I shall make you into fishers of men'. When Peter had spoken, all the others in that dark room felt great relief. They lit lamps and poured out wine and decided in which direction each one would go to start on his mission. Early the next morning, they all set off on their assignment. And then the *miracle*. Within two years, Christendom had spread all round the Mediterranean and far up towards France. Millions and millions of people were Christian and prepared to endure torture and persecution."

"Yes."

"That's how it is. That's what the miracle is like. And *that's* where I stay. Infamies occurring in the name of love are the work of man, devastating evidence of our freedom to commit every conceivable crime."

"Yes."

"Do you understand?"

"I understand."

"Communion is a confirmation and is to remind you of your affinity with the miracle."

"I'm starting at the College of Nursing next autumn."

"Oh, are you, has that been decided?"

"Yes, it's been decided. Mamma wants me to have a proper profession, so that I can stand on my own two feet and don't have to be dependent, as she calls it. Though she didn't think much of this nursing idea."

"But now it's decided?"

"When I decide something, then it becomes what I want. What are you thinking, Uncle Jacob?"

"What am I thinking? Well, you never have to say 'I love you'. But you can carry out deeds of love."

"That's just how I have imagined my life. When I'm a qualified nurse, I'll join the Mission and go to Asia. I've already spoken to Rosa André and she has put my name down, but says at the same time that I'm allowed to change my mind as I am still a minor."

"But your mother doesn't know this?"

"No, I haven't told Mamma."

In the month of May, the Fyris is a river, a great river, rapids, heaving and battering against the walls of the quays. The water is brownish-black and foaming, its sound subdued, sometimes threatening. The current under the iron bridge is swirling and impatient, hurtling along, a torrent, smelling harshly and throwing up an icy chill.

They are standing slightly apart, leaning their arms on the bridge railing and looking down into the constantly unchanging, racing mass of water. It isn't dark yet, but the lamplighter has begun his rounds. Anna has taken off her elegant hat and is holding it in her hand. Suddenly she lets it go down into the wild current, hatpin, ornamental flowers, ribbons and all. It gets caught up in a whirlpool, spins round and shoots away under the bridge.

"Did you drop your hat, Anna?"

"No, it set off by itself."

She runs over to the opposite railing and watches her ridiculously departing headgear with a laugh. Jacob is closer now, looking at his pupil with astonished appreciation.

"You let it go?"

"Yes, of course. You didn't like it, did you?"

Then she turns to him, throws her arms round his neck and buries her forehead in his chest, against the stiff material and hard buttons of his summer coat. He makes a movement to draw away, but she clings on to him . . . "No, don't, it'll soon go over, no, don't say anything, no, let me have my way, it's nothing harmful."

They stand there without moving. Jacob holds her cautiously round her back. She presses her forehead even harder against his chest . . . "no, it's good like this. Don't let's talk."

"You can't forbid me to talk, Anna."

"But I don't *want* to talk."

"But I want to talk."

"What do you want to say?"

"Well, I thought I'd just point out that the Fyris has seven bridges: Iceland Bridge, Västgöta Bridge, New Bridge, Cathedral Bridge, Iron Bridge, Hagalund Bridge and Luthagen Bridge. Seven bridges."

"Seven, like the seven deadly sins."

"Are you going to list the seven deadly sins?"

"Sloth, Pride, Anger, Gluttony, Lust, Covetousness, Envy. Was that seven?"

"That was seven. Come on now, Anna, let's go. Otherwise we'll get cold."

They stop by the abutment of the bridge and listen. They can hear the light clang of the Gunilla bell through the roar of the water.

"The Gunilla clock is striking nine. Your father will begin to wonder where you've got to."

"Mamma is already angry."

They are soon at the corner between Drottninggatan and Trädgårdsgatan.

"I won't go any further with you. We'll say goodbye here."

"Thank you. Goodnight."

But they stay standing there, he still holding her hand.

"If you don't want to go to communion, Anna, telephone me at eight o'clock tomorrow morning. I'm in my study then. Then you can tell me if you're coming or not coming."

"I'll phone. The worst of it is Mamma and our guests. And my lovely confirmation dress. You won't be able to see my confirmation dress, Uncle Jacob."

"Be serious, Anna!"

"I am serious. I'll soon start crying in all seriousness."

"Then go to your room, close the door and cry. When you've cried, you'll have made your decision."

"Is it that simple?"

"Yes, of course. That simple."

He touches her cheek and starts off quickly towards Slottsbacken and Carolina Rediviva. Nor is Anna still there. She is hurrying homewards.

FINIS

Ingmar Bergman
Fårö, June 8th, 1994